AGING ISSUES, HEALTH AND FINANCIAL ALTERNATIVES

FINANCIAL EXPLOITATION OF ELDERS

CHALLENGES AND PREVENTION EFFORTS

Aging Issues, Health and Financial Alternatives

Additional books in this series can be found on Nova's website under the Series tab.

Additional E-books in this series can be found on Nova's website under the E-book tab.

Social Issues, Justice and Status

Additional books in this series can be found on Nova's website under the Series tab.

Additional E-books in this series can be found on Nova's website under the E-book tab.

AGING ISSUES, HEALTH AND FINANCIAL ALTERNATIVES

FINANCIAL EXPLOITATION OF ELDERS

CHALLENGES AND PREVENTION EFFORTS

MAXIME FAUBERT
EDITOR

New York

For permission to use material from this book please contact us:
Telephone 631-231-7269; Fax 631-231-8175
Web Site: http://www.novapublishers.com

Additional color graphics may be available in the e-book version of this book.

Library of Congress Cataloging-in-Publication Data

ISBN: 978-1-62417-904-4

Published by Nova Science Publishers, Inc. † New York

CONTENTS

PREFACE

Elder financial exploitation is the illegal or improper use of an older adult's funds or property. It has been described as an epidemic with society-wide repercussions. While combating elder financial exploitation is largely the responsibility of state and local social service, criminal justice, and consumer protection agencies, the federal government has a role to play in this area as well. This book describes the challenges states face in preventing and responding to elder financial exploitation, as well as the actions some federal agencies have taken to help states address these challenges.

Chapter 1 – Elder financial exploitation is the illegal or improper use of an older adult's funds or property. It has been described as an epidemic with society-wide repercussions. While combating elder financial exploitation is largely the responsibility of state and local social service, criminal justice, and consumer protection agencies, the federal government has a role to play in this area as well. GAO was asked to review issues related to elder financial exploitation. This report describes the challenges states face in (1) preventing and (2) responding to elder financial exploitation, as well as the actions some federal agencies have taken to help states address these challenges.

To obtain this information, GAO interviewed state and local social service, criminal justice, and consumer protection officials in California, Illinois, New York, and Pennsylvania—states with large elderly populations; officials in seven federal agencies; and various elder abuse experts. GAO also analyzed federal strategic plans and other documents and reviewed relevant research, federal laws and regulations, and state laws.

Chapter 2 – This is the Statement of Senator Herbert Kohl. Hearing on "America's Invisible Epidemic: Preventing Elder Financial Abuse."

In: Financial Exploitation of Elders
Editor: Maxime Faubert
ISBN: 978-1-62417-904-4

Chapter 1

ELDER JUSTICE: NATIONAL STRATEGY NEEDED TO EFFECTIVELY COMBAT ELDER FINANCIAL EXPLOITATION*

United States Government Accountability Office

WHY GAO DID THIS STUDY

Elder financial exploitation is the illegal or improper use of an older adult's funds or property. It has been described as an epidemic with society-wide repercussions. While combating elder financial exploitation is largely the responsibility of state and local social service, criminal justice, and consumer protection agencies, the federal government has a role to play in this area as well. GAO was asked to review issues related to elder financial exploitation. This report describes the challenges states face in (1) preventing and (2) responding to elder financial exploitation, as well as the actions some federal agencies have taken to help states address these challenges.

To obtain this information, GAO interviewed state and local social service, criminal justice, and consumer protection officials in California, Illinois, New York, and Pennsylvania—states with large elderly populations; officials in seven federal agencies; and various elder abuse experts. GAO also

* This is an edited, reformatted and augmented version of United States Government Accountability Office, Publication No. GAO-13-110, dated November 2012.

analyzed federal strategic plans and other documents and reviewed relevant research, federal laws and regulations, and state laws.

What GAO Recommends

Federal agencies should develop a written national strategy addressing challenges GAO identified, facilitate case investigation and prosecution, and improve data, among other things. The Consumer Financial Protection Bureau and the Department of Health and Human Services supported GAO's recommendations. FTC did not believe it is necessary to examine the feasibility of requiring victim's age in complaints. GAO maintains the importance of its recommendation.

What GAO Found

Officials in each of the four states GAO contacted identified the need for more safeguards and public awareness activities to help prevent elder financial exploitation. They also noted that it is difficult to prevent exploitation by individuals such as financial services providers, power of attorney agents, guardians, and paid in-home caregivers. Although states have primary responsibility for combating elder financial exploitation, the federal government could disseminate information on model power of attorney legislation, for example, to help states better safeguard against power of attorney abuse—one type of federal activity authorized under the Older Americans Act of 1965. In addition, experts and state and local officials told GAO that many older adults need more information about what constitutes elder financial exploitation in order to report and avoid it. The seven federal agencies GAO reviewed have undertaken activities to increase public awareness of elder financial exploitation. While some experts observed that a nationwide approach to educating the public is needed, federal public awareness activities are not currently conducted as part of a broader coordinated approach, which GAO believes could help ensure the effective use of federal resources. The Elder Justice Coordinating Council, which held its first meeting in 2012, could be the vehicle for developing and implementing a coordinated national strategy. The Council is composed of officials from federal agencies and is charged with developing national priorities and coordinating federal elder justice activities.

Experts and officials in each state GAO reviewed indicated that difficulty 1) gaining expertise, 2) sustaining collaboration between law enforcement and adult protective services agencies, and 3) obtaining data hinders their response to elder financial exploitation. As with prevention, many federal agencies have individually taken steps to address these challenges that are in line with their own missions. For example, the Department of Justice (Justice) has begun to construct a website that contains training and other materials prosecutors can use to build their expertise in investigating and prosecuting elder abuse, which includes elder financial exploitation. However, there are gaps in federal support in some areas. For example, law enforcement officials in each of the four states GAO reviewed indicated that it is not clear how they should obtain the federal support they need to respond to interstate and international cases. Justice can provide this information, in keeping with its priority to strengthen its relationship with state and local law enforcement. Similarly, the Federal Trade Commission's (FTC) Consumer Sentinel Network database compiles incidents of financial exploitation reported to it by many sources around the country but receives incidents from state government agencies in only 12 states. The database would be of greater use if FTC obtained incidents from more of the states and contained an indicator that the incident involved an older adult.

ABBREVIATIONS

AoA	Administration on Aging
APS	Adult protective services
CFPB	Bureau of Consumer Financial Protection (commonly referred to as the Consumer Financial Protection Bureau)
CDAA	California District Attorneys Association
	Consumer Sentinel Consumer Sentinel Network database
HHS	Department of Health and Human Services
Justice	Department of Justice
EFPN	Elder Financial Protection Network
EJA	Elder Justice Act of 2009
EJCC	Elder Justice Coordinating Council
FTC	Federal Trade Commission

FinCEN	Financial Crimes Enforcement Network
FINRA	Financial Industry Regulatory Authority
NASAA	North American Securities Administrators
NCEA	National Center on Elder Abuse
Office for Older Americans	Office for the Financial Protection of Older Americans
OAA	Older Americans Act of 1965
RFPA	Right to Financial Privacy Act of 1978
SEC	Securities and Exchange Commission
SAR	Suspicious Activity Report

November 15, 2012
Congressional Requesters

Elder financial exploitation is the illegal or improper use of an older adult's funds, property, or assets.[1] Experts have described it as an epidemic with society-wide repercussions. Perpetrators may be family members; paid home care workers; those with fiduciary responsibilities, such as financial advisors or legal guardians; or strangers who inundate older adults with mail, telephone, or Internet scams. Older adults are particularly vulnerable to financial exploitation because, as research has shown, financial decision-making ability decreases with age. Moreover, older adults are often ashamed to report exploitation or even admit that they have been exploited because they are afraid of losing their independence. As a result, existing data on elder financial exploitation may substantially underestimate its extent.

Elder financial exploitation has far-reaching effects on its victims in particular and society in general. A study of media reports from April to June 2010 estimated that financial exploitation cost older adults at least $2.9 billion in 2010. [2] The money that older adults lose in these cases is rarely recovered, and the loss can undermine both the health of older adults and their ability to support or care for themselves. Consequently, the burden of caring for exploited older adults may fall on various state and federal programs. For example, a review of 80 elder financial exploitation cases in Utah in 2010 found the state's Medicaid program would potentially have to pay about $900,000 to cover the cost of care for older adults in that state who had suffered substantial losses.[3]

As the U.S. population ages, growing numbers of older adults could be at risk of financial exploitation, so its potential impact on society is likely to increase. Combating elder financial exploitation is primarily the responsibility of state and local agencies. At the same time, however, multiple federal agencies have a role to play in supporting state and local efforts. In light of these growing concerns, we were asked to provide information on elder financial exploitation issues. Specifically, this report addresses the challenges states face in (1) preventing and (2) responding to elder financial exploitation, as well as the actions some federal agencies have taken to help states address these challenges.

To address these objectives, we interviewed officials from agencies that included state and local social services, criminal justice, and consumer protection agencies in California, Illinois, New York, and Pennsylvania. We selected these states to achieve variation in location, because of the large size of their elder population, and because each state had a number of initiatives to combat elder financial exploitation. Across the four states, we held interviews with representatives from entities such as state and local adult protective services (APS) agencies; offices of attorneys general; police and sheriffs' departments; local district attorneys and courts; and state banking, securities, and insurance regulators. In three of the four states we also spoke with private organizations that work on issues related to elder financial exploitation, such as a university research center, elder abuse forensic center, and state banking association. In Pennsylvania, we met with experts from the Institute on Protective Services at Temple University and also attended an elder financial exploitation training for APS workers that was hosted by the Institute. We focused only on financial exploitation of older adults living at home, not on older adults in long-term care facilities.

We also interviewed experts in the field of elder abuse—including academics and practitioners—and representatives from a variety of nonprofit and private sector organizations, such as the AARP, American Bar Association, and American Bankers Association. We interviewed representatives from University of California at Irvine's Center of Excellence on Elder Abuse and Neglect and the University of Kentucky's Justice Center for Elders and Vulnerable Adults. In addition, in order to gain the perspectives of large national and small community banks, we interviewed officials at six financial institutions. These banks are not, however, representative of banks nationwide. Furthermore, we interviewed officials and analyzed strategic plans and other documents from seven federal agencies—including the Administration on Aging (AoA) within the Department of Health and Human Services (HHS), Bureau of Consumer Financial Protection (commonly referred to as the Consumer Financial Protection Bureau or CFPB),

Department of Justice (Justice), Federal Trade Commission (FTC), Financial Crimes Enforcement Network (FinCEN) within the Department of the Treasury, Postal Inspection Service, and Securities and Exchange Commission (SEC). In total, we held dozens of interviews with experts and officials from federal, state, local, and non-governmental organizations. We also reviewed relevant federal laws and regulations, as well as selected state laws. Moreover, we attended the initial meeting of members of the Elder Justice Coordinating Council (EJCC), which includes officials from 11 federal agencies with an interest in elder abuse. We also attended several conferences related to elder financial exploitation, including the American Society on Aging's 2012 Aging in America Conference, California District Attorneys Association's (CDAA) 2011 Elder Abuse Symposium, Stanford Center on Longevity and the Financial Industry Regulatory Authority's (FINRA) 2011 State and Future of Financial Fraud Conference, Elder Financial Protection Network's (EFPN) 2012 Call to Action Conference, and a 2011 webcast on elder issues hosted by the Nebraska Department of Health and Human Services and State Bar Association's 2011 Elder Issues Webcast. At the CDAA Symposium, we held small group meetings with district attorneys and investigators from various counties in California. And at the EFPN Conference we held a small group meeting with local district attorneys, advocates, a state insurance agency official, and a financial institution.

To illustrate the complexities of combating elder exploitation, we met with a social service agency, several criminal justice agencies, and, in one case, a family member to develop detailed case histories on six prosecuted cases of elder financial exploitation. The perpetrators in these cases were family members, financial services providers, or telephone scammers. We identified cases from news stories and internet searches. We selected six cases because they (1) occurred in three of our four review states (California, New York, and Pennsylvania), (2) involved each of the different types of elder financial exploitation (exploitation by family or trusted others, exploitation by financial services providers, and exploitation by strangers), and (3) included instances where more than one agency or system was involved. The cases we selected are a non-generalizable sample of elder financial exploitation cases.

Lastly, we identified and reviewed research published from 2000 onward on elder financial abuse or elder financial exploitation by searching numerous bibliographic databases and reviewing materials cited by elder abuse experts or published by federal, state, and non-governmental organizations. We focused our review on published research on the extent, impact, cost, and nature of elder financial exploitation. We also interviewed an official from the

Utah Division of Aging and Adult Services to discuss the state's study on the cost of elder financial exploitation.

We conducted this performance audit from November 2011 to November 2012 in accordance with generally accepted government auditing standards. Those standards require that we plan and perform the audit to obtain sufficient, appropriate evidence to provide a reasonable basis for our findings and conclusions based on our audit objectives. We believe that the evidence obtained provides a reasonable basis for our findings and conclusions based on our audit objectives. Our investigative activities were conducted in accordance with standards prescribed by the Council of the Inspectors General for Integrity and Efficiency.

BACKGROUND

Elder financial exploitation, one type of elder abuse, can occur in conjunction with, and might lead to other types of elder abuse.[4] Financial exploitation of older adults can take many forms and perpetrators can include family members, friends, legal guardians, paid caregivers, and strangers. Table 1 provides some examples.

Table 1. Examples of Forms of Elder Financial Exploitation by Type of Perpetrator

Perpetrators	Forms
Family members, friends, in-home caregivers, legal guardians, representative payeesa, etc.	—Theft of cash or other valuables —Withdrawals from bank accounts or use of credit cards —Transfer of deeds —Misuse of an older adult's power of attorney —Misappropriation of an incapacitated older adult's income or assets —Identity theft
Financial services providers (brokers, financial advisors, insurance agents, or others in the financial services industry)	—Sale of fraudulent investments (Ponzi or pyramid schemes) —Sale of financial products or services unsuitable for an older adult'scircumstances, such as long-term annuities
Strangers	—Lottery, mail, telephone, or Internet scams —Door-to-door home repair scams —Identity theft

Source: GAO analysis of published research.

[a]Representative payees are persons who receive Social Security benefits on behalf of recipients who are determined to be incapable of managing their finances. 20 C.F.R. §§ 416.601 and 416.2001.

Older adults are particularly attractive targets for financial exploitation by unscrupulous individuals. As a group, older adults tend to possess more wealth than those who are younger because they have had a longer time to acquire it. In addition, the incidence of Alzheimer's disease and other dementias that undermine judgment increases with age.[5] Moreover, financial capacity—the capacity to manage money and financial assets in ways that meet one's needs—generally declines with age, and this decline may go unaddressed until it is too late.[6] State and local agencies in the social services, criminal justice, and consumer protection systems in each state are at the forefront of efforts to prevent, detect, and respond to elder financial exploitation. Seven federal agencies whose missions correspond to the state and local social service, criminal justice, and consumer protection systems are positioned to contribute to state and local efforts in this area: AoA, CFPB, Justice, FTC, FinCEN, SEC, and the Postal Inspection Service (see fig. 1). [7]

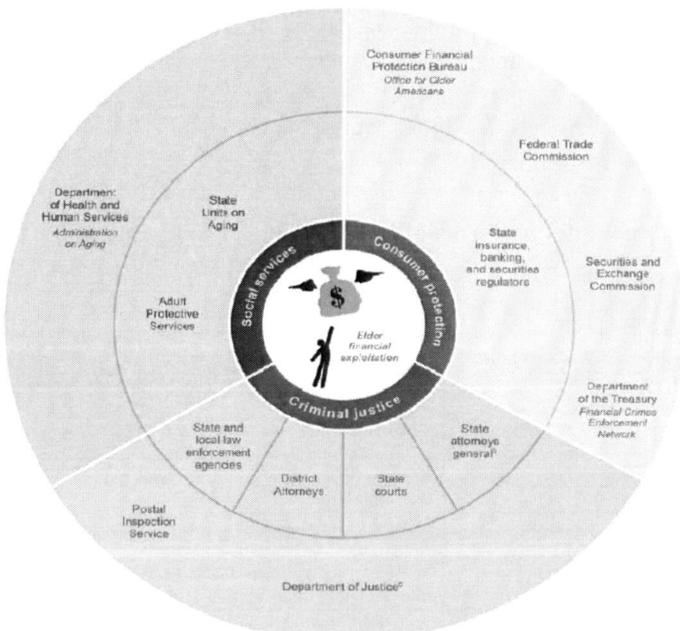

[a] The relationship between the federal and the state and local agencies in a given system varies.

[b] State attorneys general also play a consumer protection role.

[c] Justice also plays a consumer protection role.

Figure 1. State and Federal Systems and Agencies Positioned to Combat Elder Financial Exploitation.[a]

At the state and local level, APS agencies investigate and substantiate reports of suspected elder abuse, including financial exploitation and, if the client agrees to accept help, can arrange for services to secure their safety and meet their basic needs. APS can also refer cases to law enforcement agencies or district attorneys for criminal investigation and prosecution. Whether an elder financial exploitation case comes to the attention of criminal justice authorities through referral from APS or some other means, law enforcement agencies and district attorneys can exercise broad discretion when deciding if a case warrants any action on their part.

State-level consumer protection agencies—such as banking, securities, and insurance regulators—conduct examinations to ensure that rules to protect consumers are followed and take enforcement actions against institutions that break the rules. State attorneys general may also prosecute cases or respond to consumer protection inquiries.

Although combating elder financial abuse is explicitly included in the mission of only one federal agency, CFPB's Office for the Financial Protection of Older Americans (Office for Older Americans), it is implicit in the mission of others that work to combat elder abuse, protect consumers or investors, or prevent fraud (see fig. 2).

Federal legislation has established a foundation for the federal government to assume a leadership role in combating elder abuse, including elder financial exploitation, and basis for greater coordination across federal agencies in this area. The Older Americans Act of 1965 (OAA)[8] requires AoA to develop objectives, priorities, policy, and a longterm plan for

- facilitating the development, implementation, and continuous improvement of a coordinated, multidisciplinary elder justice system in the United States;
- promoting collaborative efforts and diminishing duplicative efforts in the development and carrying out of elder justice programs at the federal, state, and local levels;
- establishing an information clearinghouse to collect, maintain, and disseminate information concerning best practices and resources for training, technical assistance, and other activities to assist states and communities to carry out evidence-based programs to prevent and address elder abuse, neglect, and exploitation;
- working with states, Justice, and other federal agencies to annually collect, maintain, and disseminate data on elder abuse, neglect, and exploitation, to the extent practicable;

- establishing federal guidelines and disseminating best practices for uniform data collection and reporting by states;
- conducting research on elder abuse, neglect, and exploitation; and
- carrying out a study to determine the extent of elder abuse, neglect, and exploitation in all settings.[9]

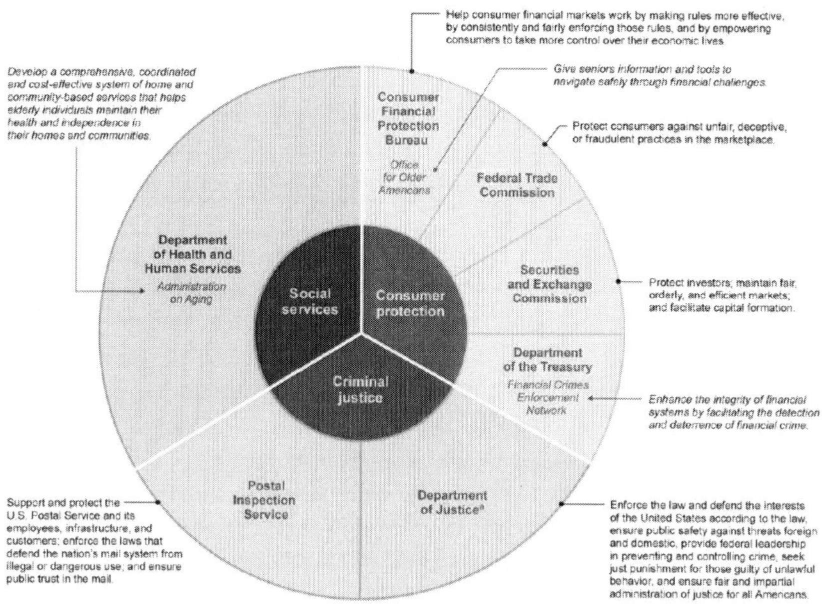

[a]Justice also plays a consumer protection role. Specifically, two of Justice's strategic objectives are to (1) prevent and intervene in crimes against vulnerable populations; uphold the rights of, and improve services to, America's crime victims; and (2) combat corruption, economic crimes, and international organized crime.

Figure 2. Federal Agencies with Missions That Involve Combating Elder Financial Exploitation.

The Elder Justice Act of 2009 (EJA)[10] contains provisions pertaining to APS as well as elder justice, in general. It authorizes funding for

- HHS to
  - annually collect and disseminate data regarding elder abuse, neglect, and exploitation of elders in coordination with Justice;[11]

- develop and disseminate information on best practices and provide training for carrying out adult protective services;[12]
- conduct research related to the provision of adult protective services;[13]
- provide technical assistance to states and others that provide or fund the provision of adult protective services;[14] and
- establish 10 elder abuse, neglect, and exploitation forensic centers, in consultation with Justice, that would (1) conduct research on forensic markers for elder abuse, neglect, or exploitation, and methodologies for determining when and how health care, emergency, social and protective, and legal service providers should intervene and when these cases should be reported to law enforcement; (2) develop forensic expertise regarding elder abuse, neglect, and exploitation; and (3) use the data they have collected to develop, in coordination with Justice, the capacity of geriatric health care professionals and law enforcement authorities to collect forensic evidence, including evidence needed to determine if elder abuse, neglect, or exploitation has occurred.[15]

- Grants to state and local governments for demonstration projects that test methods and training to detect or prevent elder abuse or financial exploitation;[16] and
- An Elder Justice Coordinating Council and an Advisory Board on Elder Abuse, Neglect, and Exploitation to develop priorities for the elder justice field, coordinate federal activities, and provide recommendations to Congress.[17]

Currently, the Elder Justice Coordinating Council consists of the following federal agencies: Consumer Financial Protection Bureau, Corporation for National and Community Service,[18] Department of Health and Human Services, Department of Housing and Urban Development, Department of Justice, Department of Labor, Department of the Treasury, Department of Veterans Affairs, Federal Trade Commission, Postal Inspection Service, and Social Security Administration.

Coordination among federal agencies is also a feature of the Dodd-Frank Wall Street Reform and Consumer Protection Act, which established CFPB, requiring it to coordinate its consumer protection efforts of older adults with other federal agencies.[19] CFPB's Office for Older Americans is charged with facilitating the financial literacy of seniors on protection from unfair, deceptive, and abusive practices and on current and future financial choices.[20]

STATES IDENTIFIED THE NEED FOR MORE SAFEGUARDS AND PUBLIC AWARENESS ACTIVITIES TO PREVENT ELDER FINANCIAL EXPLOITATION

States Cited Need for More Safeguards to Prevent Elder Financial Exploitation

According to officials in the four states we visited, financial exploitation of older adults by financial services providers, power of attorney agents, and in-home caregivers is particularly difficult to prevent.[21]

Financial Services Providers

Older adults may consult with a variety of financial professionals, such as financial planners,[22] broker-dealers,[23] and insurance agents.[24] However, older adults, similar to other consumers, may lack the information to make sound decisions about choosing a financial services provider and protecting their assets from exploitation. As a result, they may unknowingly put themselves at risk of financial exploitation.

Individuals who present themselves as financial planners may adopt a variety of titles and designations. In some cases, privately conferred designations—such as Certified Financial Planner®—require formal certification procedures, including examinations and continuing professional education credits, while other designations may merely signify that membership dues have been paid. Designations that imply expertise in advising older adults have been a source of particular concern among state securities regulators, according to the North American Securities Administrators Association (NASAA).[25] Older adults may lack information to distinguish among the various senior specific designations. Indeed, in 2011, we reported that there is some confusion about what these titles mean and the level of skill required to obtain them.[26]

Another concern is that older adults may be fooled by investment professionals who use questionable tactics to market financial products, such as “free lunch seminars” at which financial professionals seek to sell financial products to older adults during a free meal. SEC, the Financial Industry

Regulatory Authority (FINRA), and NASAA examined 110 firms that sponsored free lunch seminars from April 2006 to June 2007 offered in seven states and found that 63 seminars used misleading advertising and sales materials, 25 seminars resulted in unsuitable recommendations, and in 14 seminars there were fraudulent practices used, such as selling fictitious investments.[27]

Exploitation by "Senior Specialist"

Calling himself a senior financial advisor, an insurance agent licensed in California met an 89-year-old partially blind, intermittently confused man at a senior center. The agent persuaded him to invest about $250,000 in a flexible premium deferred annuity, warning him not to let anyone talk him out of it. As a result, the man was left with no penalty-free access to his entire life savings for the next 11 years, while the agent earned a commission on this transaction. To earn about $16,000 more in commissions, the agent then convinced the man to move half the amount invested in the annuity into unregistered stock, which cost the man a surrender fee of about $10,000. The stock turned out to be worthless, leaving the man with a fraction of what he had when he met the agent. Attempts by the man's nephew to retrieve his uncle's money were unsuccessful. The nephew reported the insurance agent to the California Department of Insurance, which eventually revoked the agent's license, but local police did not pursue the older adult's case. While the insurance agent faced no criminal charges in this case, he was later sentenced to 3 years in prison for defrauding another older adult.

Preventing the sale of unsuitable or fraudulent investments to older adults is difficult.[28] An investment can be unsuitable for an older adult if it has features that might not provide its intended benefit during the investor's lifetime. Older adults also can be sold what they believe to be legitimate investments, but are actually completely fraudulent products that hold little or no value.

SEC has developed some educational materials and SEC and CFPB have conducted research related to investment fraud that targets older adults. For example, SEC has published a guide for older adults that counsels them to check their investment adviser's disciplinary history, lists warning signs of fraud, and provides information on where to go for help.[29] SEC also provides a link to a FINRA website that provides consumers with the required qualifications, including educational requirements, of the designations used by securities professionals.

In August 2012, SEC released a study on financial literacy among investors and stated the agency's desire to develop a strategy for increasing the financial literacy of certain groups, including older adults. CFPB plans to issue a report in early 2013 to Congress and the SEC that will address providing information to older adults about financial advisors and their credentials. In June 2012, the CFPB issued a public inquiry for information about elder financial exploitation, including a question on what resources older adults have to determine the legitimacy, value, and authenticity of credentials held by investment professionals.[30] CFPB expects to share its results in 2013.

Investment Fraud Using a "Ponzi" Scheme

The founder and president of a real estate and financial consulting firm convinced around 200 individuals—about one-third of whom were older adults—to invest in real estate projects that failed to generate any significant revenue. He also convinced them to obtain reverse mortgages on their homes, and to invest the proceeds with his firm. The investments turned out to be a "Ponzi" scheme. Specifically, the perpetrator paid distributions to some investors from others' deposits; misled investors with false amortization schedules; and used investors' money to pay for his Porsche, mortgage, and other personal expenses. The scheme was reported to FINRA, investigated by the FBI, and prosecuted by the Eastern District of New York U.S. Attorney's Office, which sought sentencing enhancements for targeting the elderly. Victims lost over $12 million.

They also reported irreplaceable financial losses, emotional distress, feelings of betrayal and disbelief, and various physical symptoms as a result.

Power of Attorney

Older adults can use a legal document referred to as a financial power of attorney to appoint another person (an agent) to manage their finances should they become incapable of doing so. Having a financial power of attorney enables an older adult (a principal) to choose the person who can legally make these decisions for them, when needed.

Powers of attorney are easy for anyone to create, can vary in specificity and format, and do not require legal assistance or a court for execution. Each of the four states we contacted has a law that helps prevent misuse of powers of attorney by specifying the responsibilities of agents and, in at least one, penalties for misuse. However, powers of attorney can be forged or perhaps otherwise improperly obtained without a principal's knowledge or consent and an agent can easily use the principal's money for his or her own benefit.

For this reason, many state and local officials we interviewed in the four states were concerned about misuse of these instruments. For example, one Pennsylvania official described power of attorney documents as a "powerful, simple, and dangerous tool."

Power of Attorney Abuse

A month after an elderly man with dementia and his wife agreed to add their daughter's name to their bank account, the daughter convinced her mother to sign a document providing her financial power of attorney. When the woman signed, she was in the hospital for a broken hip and a stroke and later claimed she was heavily medicated.

Over the next 3 months, the daughter placed the deed to her parent's home in her name, wrote checks on their account totaling nearly $600,000 that were never questioned by the bank, and attempted to withdraw about $500,000 more. When the woman's son discovered what had been happening, he had the bank stop payment on the $500,000 and asked the local district attorney to investigate.

The daughter was charged with numerous counts of theft, pled guilty, and was sentenced to 3 years probation. The deed was transferred back to the woman and although the prosecutor sought restitution, the $600,000 was not recoverable—it had been used to pay off the daughter's mortgage, country club membership, and other bills.

Some APS and criminal justice officials we spoke to indicated that stronger state power of attorney laws could help prevent elder financial exploitation by agents.

For example, Pennsylvania officials said that current state laws have been ineffective at (1) creating practices to monitor the activities of power of attorney agents and (2) encouraging banks to question power of attorney documents they find questionable. In California, law enforcement officials noted that notaries were not always held accountable for their role in signing power of attorney documents.

To help strengthen state laws designed to prevent misuse of financial powers of attorney, the Uniform Law Commission[31] has developed the Uniform Power of Attorney Act, which

- explicitly defines the duties of the power of attorney agent, including fiduciary duties such as acting in good faith and keeping careful records;
- allows a third party to refuse to honor a power of attorney agreement if there is a good faith belief that the principal may be subject to abuse, and requires the third party to report to APS;
- allows co-agents to be appointed for additional third-party oversight; and
- imposes liability on agents who violate the law.

According to the Uniform Law Commission, 13 states have adopted the entire Uniform Power of Attorney Act.[32] Others have enacted various other power of attorney laws. For example, New York requires an agent to provide a full accounting to APS when it is investigating a report that the principal may be in need of protective or other services or the victim of abuse or neglect. If it is not provided within 15 days, APS can commence a special proceeding to compel the production of the information. Illinois has added safeguards for principals to its law and created additional court remedies for violations of the law. However, according to the Uniform Law Commission, a number of states have made no changes to laws governing powers of attorney since the Uniform Power of Attorney Act was published. Powers of attorney are generally regulated under state, not federal, law; however, AoA and CFPB are providing some information to states and power of attorney agents to help prevent power of attorney abuse. The AoA-supported National Legal Resource Center co-sponsors trainings for states on the adoption of the Uniform Power of Attorney Act. Furthermore, the CFPB is developing a guide to educate "lay fiduciaries"—including guardians and agents under powers of attorney—about their responsibilities, and is planning to develop several state-specific lay fiduciary guides, scheduled for release in 2013.

Guardians

There are limited safeguards to protect older adults from abuse by guardians, who are granted authority by a state court to make decisions in the best interest of an incapacitated individual concerning his or her person or property. While guardians can play a key role in managing the assets of these older adults, we have noted in past reports that guardians are only subject to limited safeguards that could protect these older adults from financial exploitation. For example, local officials in California noted that it can be hard to determine whether a person applying to be a guardian is doing so to further his ward's best interests. We have also reported that few states conduct criminal background checks on potential guardians. Moreover, we have noted concerns with weak court oversight of appointed guardians, as well as poor communication between the courts and federal agencies that have enabled guardians to chronically abuse their wards and/or others.[33]

Caregivers

Exploitation by in-home caregivers was also cited by local APS officials, police, and district attorneys we spoke to as a type of abuse that is difficult to prevent. These caregivers range from personal care aides who provide non-medical assistance such as helping with laundry and cooking, to home health aides who check an older adult's vital signs or assist with medical equipment. In-home caregivers may be employed by a private company approved to provide services via a state's OAA [34] program or independently hired by older adults or their families. Caregiver services may also be covered under a state Medicaid program if the individual is eligible for Medicaid.[35] Older adults may rely on and trust in-home caregivers, and some caregivers have used that relationship to exploit their clients.[36] For example, a caregiver may be given access to an older adult's ATM or credit card to help with banking or grocery shopping and later be found withdrawing money or purchasing items for themselves. As the population ages and public policies encourage older adults to remain in their homes for as long as practical, there will be an increased need for in-home caregivers. States are responsible for protecting older adults from exploitation by in-home caregivers, and safeguards vary by state. Police and district attorneys we interviewed were concerned that in-home caregivers are subject to limited, if any, background checks. A California law enforcement official told us that caregivers suspected of exploiting older adults sometimes have a history of theft. While the Medicaid program requires states to develop and implement home care provider qualification standards, there is no federal Medicaid requirement for criminal background checks.[37] According to the National Conference of State Legislatures, while many states have required agencies to conduct background checks before employing in-home caregivers who are paid by Medicaid or with other state funds, these laws vary greatly in their breadth and scope and the amount of flexibility afforded the agencies when they use the checks to make hiring decisions.[38] Napa County,

California recently initiated an innovative paid in-home caregiver screening initiative. Before in-home caregivers can work in that county, they must submit to a background check and obtain a permit annually.[39] While background checks for in-home caregivers help flag potential abusers, an AARP study has found that states do not always use all available federal, state, and local criminal data systems. For one, the implementation cost may discourage their use. Moreover, their effectiveness in reducing elder abuse, in general, is unproven.[40] As required by the Patient Protection and Affordable Care Act of 2010,[41] the Centers for Medicare and Medicaid Services implemented the National Background Check Program that encourages states to adopt safeguards to protect clients of in-home caregivers. This voluntary program provides grants to states to conduct background checks for employees of longterm care facilities and providers, such as home health agencies and personal care service providers. As of November 2012, 19 states were participating. The results of this program could provide data on the effectiveness of background checks in preventing elder abuse, including elder financial exploitation.[42] State and local authorities in the four states we visited told us current safeguards are not always sufficient to prevent exploitation by those older adults depend on for assistance. Although states are generally responsible for laws and regulations regarding these issues, the OAA directs the federal government to disseminate information about best practices to prevent elder abuse, including elder financial exploitation. According to our analysis, there is a role for the federal government to provide more information and guidance to prevent these types of elder financial exploitation.

State and Federal Officials Called for Greater Focus on Public Awareness

Experts and federal, state, and local officials told us that older adults need more information about what constitutes elder financial exploitation in order to know how to avoid it.[43] However, APS and law enforcement officials told us that it is difficult for them to reach many older adults with this message and that they have little funding to promote public awareness. For example, in one California county officials reported that due to budget cuts, they had lost many positions that involved educating the public about elder financial exploitation. Each of the seven federal agencies we reviewed independently produces and disseminates public information on elder financial exploitation that is tailored to its own mission.

Table 2. Selected Public Awareness Efforts of Federal Agencies Related to Elder Financial Exploitation

Agency	Public Awareness Efforts
CFPB	Office for Older Americans provides information for the public on its website about how to avoid being exploited. Published a guide for consumers about reverse mortgages.
FTC	Produces publications, pamphlets, and videos on a range of consumer protection issues, such as telemarketing fraud, and distributes them via its website, the media, and partnering organizations. Piloted a partnership with the AARP Foundation that funds peer counseling for older adults or their relatives who think they have been victimized. Works with AoA's Senior Medicare Patrols to distribute educational materials to older adults and collect complaints.
AoA	Distributes an e-newsletter discussing elder abuse, including financial exploitation. Maintains Senior Legal Helplines. Provides elder abuse prevention grants. Collaborates with nonprofit Women's Center for a Secure Retirement to provide a gateway for financial information for women.
Justice	Provides grants to states, localities, and nonprofits for elder abuse prevention activities, including education and public awareness campaigns. Provides information through its public websites on how individuals can protect themselves from and report various types of financial fraud.
SEC	Distributes investor information that may relate to elder financial exploitation via its website, hotline, pamphlets, and regional events. Provides an investment fraud guide for older adults. Produces investor alert bulletins. Works with AARP, FINRA, and state securities regulators on the Outsmarting Investment Fraud campaign.
FinCEN	Provides the public with information via its website on scams and resources for victims of fraud or identity theft.
Postal Inspection Service	Deployed FakeChecks.org Campaign in 2007 to target international fraud schemes that are often directed toward older adults. In 2010, sent a postcard containing information about preventing fraud, including elder financial exploitation,to every U.S. household. Participated in AARP Town Hall meeting in 2011. Conducts ongoing fraud prevention messaging on its website. Makes community presentations on how to avoid scams during National Consumer Protection Week each March (with FTC).

Source: GAO analysis of agency documents and interviews.

For example, SEC produces information to educate investors about fraud prevention, including an investment guide for older adults. FTC publishes information to protect consumers, and AoA disseminates information to help reduce elder abuse, including elder financial exploitation. (See table 2 for examples of the types of information provided by each of these agencies.) These seven agencies have also worked together at times to increase public awareness of elder financial exploitation. For example, each year FTC and the Postal Inspection Service collaborate on community presentations during National Consumer Protection Week. However, although the OAA calls for a coordinated federal elder justice system,[44] which includes educating the public, the seven agencies we reviewed do not conduct these activities as part of a broader coordinated approach. In previous work, we found that agencies can use limited funding more efficiently by coordinating their activities and can strengthen their collaboration by establishing joint strategies.[45] Similar calls for coordination were raised when the EJCC held its first meeting on October 11, 2012, to begin implementing its mandate to coordinate federal elder justice activities and develop national priorities. As EJCC Chairman, the Secretary of HHS stated that combating elder abuse—which includes elder financial exploitation—is an "all-of-government" effort and that federal programs are not organized in a strategic way, which decreases their effectiveness. One expert noted that there is a clear need for a strategic, multi-faceted public awareness campaign on elder abuse. An official from the Financial Services Roundtable[46] added that many agencies are trying to focus on awareness and education, but their efforts appear unorganized and uncoordinated.

Difficulty Gaining Expertise, Sustaining Collaboration, and Obtaining Data Hinders States' Responses to Elder Financial Exploitation

Special Knowledge and Skills Are Needed to Respond to Elder Financial Exploitation

According to state and local officials we spoke with in four states, effectively investigating and prosecuting elder financial exploitation requires special skills and knowledge, which APS workers, law enforcement officers, and district attorneys sometimes lack. For example, APS officials noted that some case workers have little background or training in investigating financial crimes, and would find it difficult to respond to these cases. Local law enforcement officials also noted that they receive little training on elder financial exploitation and need additional training to build expertise. In addition, we were told that some prosecutors and judges are reluctant to take on cases of suspected elder financial exploitation because of competing priorities and limited resources, a continuing belief that elder financial exploitation is primarily a civil issue, or a view of older adult victims as unreliable witnesses.

State and local officials in the four states we reviewed are attempting to increase their expertise.[47] For example, some state and local officials told us they attempt to acquire investigative expertise through formal and on-the-job training, by dedicating units or staff to investigate suspected cases of elder financial exploitation, or by contracting for assistance from certified fraud examiners or other forensic accountants.[48]

However, state and local officials also told us that funding constraints limited their ability to build this additional expertise. Moreover, officials and experts told us that in order to more effectively allocate their limited resources, state and local entities would need more information about which practices have proven to be most effective for investigating, as well as preventing, elder financial exploitation.

AoA and Justice have developed some resources that could be used to help state and local agencies build expertise in identifying, investigating, and prosecuting elder financial exploitation (see table 3).

Under the EJA, HHS is authorized to develop and disseminate best practices and provide training for APS workers,[49] and AoA-supported resource centers compile information about elder abuse in general for easy access. However, information pertaining specifically to elder financial exploitation topics—such as mass marketing fraud, power of attorney abuse, or investment fraud—may be dated or more difficult to find because it is intermingled with other materials.[50]

For example, AoA's National Center on Elder Abuse (NCEA) has compiled a list of elder abuse training materials from a variety of sources, but we could find no quick and clear way to identify which trainings cover financial exploitation.

Additionally, Justice officials told us that it would be beneficial for more training to be available to prosecutors of elder abuse. Justice has identified providing training and resources to combat elder abuse as a strategy to achieve its objective of preventing and intervening in crimes against vulnerable populations. Justice officials indicated that they are developing an elder justice prosecution website that could serve as a resource and help build expertise. The website is expected to consolidate training materials in use across the country, primary litigation materials from local district attorneys, and information from relevant academic centers, such as the University of California at Irvine and Stanford University. However, it is unclear when this project will be completed, as Justice officials are waiting for materials from local district attorneys. As a result, prosecutors and other law enforcement officials currently do not have access to these materials.

Table 3. Examples of AoA and Justice Resources That Could Be Used to Increase State and Local Expertise about Elder Financial Exploitation

Agency	Resource
AoA	National Center on Elder Abuse website has materials on elder abuse, including elder financial exploitation. AoA makes formula grants to states and territories under Title VII of the Older Americans Act that are used to fund training.[a] National Adult Protective Services Resource Center provides information and technical assistance aimed at APS professionals. National Legal Resource Center provides training and information on legal issues affecting older adults. Model Approaches to Statewide Legal Assistance Systems demonstration program includes two elder abuse projects that focus on elder financial exploitation.
Justice	Funding the development of APS elder abuse training modules. Justice's Office on Violence Against Women, Office for Victims of Crime, and Bureau of Justice Assistance fund a number of trainings—including some material devoted to elder financial exploitation—to law enforcement and others inthe field each year. Prosecutors in the Criminal Division's Fraud Section have provided training at national conferences on elder fraud. Created an elder financial exploitation guide for police officers. Plans to fund the development of online training for legal aid attorneys on identifying and responding to elder abuse, including financial exploitation. Developing strategies and best practices for financial fraud and identity theft investigations.

Source: GAO analysis of HHS and Justice materials and interviews.

[a] 42 U.S.C. §§ 3058b and 3058i.

States Identified Additional Federal Support Needed to Sustain Crucial Collaborations across Systems and Levels of Government

Collaboration between APS and Criminal Justice Systems

The OAA requires AoA to develop a plan for promoting collaborative efforts to support elder justice programs at all levels.[51] Officials we met from state and local social service and criminal justice agencies in three of the four states we reviewed said that while collaboration between their systems is important for combating elder financial exploitation, collaborating can sometimes be difficult because the two systems differ in the way they respond to exploitation and carry out their work. Specifically, APS focuses on protecting and supporting the victim, and criminal justice focuses on prosecuting and convicting exploiters. However, according to experts, by working together, APS, the criminal justice system, and other partners can more easily accomplish both of these goals.[52] Experts have noted that some type of multidisciplinary response to elder abuse— including elder financial exploitation—is prudent because of the complex nature of the problems faced by victims and the wide variety of responses required to help them and to prosecute exploiters. In each of the four states we reviewed, local initiatives helped bridge the gap between APS and criminal justice agencies.[53] In some locations APS, criminal justice agencies, and other public and private entities have formed groups that meet periodically to develop awareness activities, foster information sharing, and discuss and resolve individual cases. Some multidisciplinary groups discuss elder abuse broadly, such as elder abuse task forces in some Pennsylvania counties and multidisciplinary groups in New York City. Others concentrate on financial exploitation specifically, such as the Philadelphia Financial Exploitation Task Force, and Financial Abuse Specialist Teams in some California counties.

Although multidisciplinary groups responding to elder financial exploitation already exist in each of the four states we visited and elsewhere, forming and sustaining these groups continues to be challenging, according to law enforcement officials in one state we visited and experts. Busy schedules and competing priorities make it difficult for some participants to attend meetings regularly, and a group's focus influences how extensively members are willing to participate. For example, in one location officials told us that when the primary focus of their group shifted from prosecuting cases to providing services, participation by law enforcement officials declined. Collaborative efforts can also be undermined by a history of poor interaction between member organizations, differences in systemic understanding of elder financial exploitation, difficulties communicating across disciplines, different understandings of limits on information sharing, unclear roles, and failure to address the group's long-term survival. 54 However, information on relevant promising practices in this area could help promote creation of such groups—particularly when resources are limited—and ensure their success.

Federal agencies have made some efforts to promote and inform collaboration between the APS and criminal justice systems in states. However, agencies have taken few steps to compile or disseminate promising practices in creating or sustaining multidisciplinary groups responding to elder financial exploitation, even though the OAA requires AoA to develop and disseminate information on best practices for adult protective services. AoA and Justice have offered a small number of grants to states to combat elder abuse or other crimes that require or encourage collaborative efforts such as multidisciplinary teams (see Table 4).

Table 4. Examples of Federal Grants That Encourage Collaboration among State Agencies That Respond to Elder Abuse

Agency	Grant
AoA	Elder Abuse Prevention Interventions Program: Requires grantees to have a partnership that includes at least the APS and criminal justice systems. AoA expected to award between $625,000 and $1.02 million each to 5-8 grantees in 2012.
	Elder Justice Community Collaborations: Relatively small ($10,000) grants specifically for setting up elder justice coalitions were awarded to over 40 grantees from 2007 to 2010.
	Prevention of Elder Abuse, Neglect, and Exploitation (OAA Title VII-A3), formula grants to all states and territories that broadly require collaboration between social services and criminal justice systems.
	Attorneys funded by Title IIIB of the Older Americans Act may work with APS in various situations, including situations dealing with guardianship issues.
	Funding from AoA's Model Approaches to Statewide Legal Assistance Systems demonstration grants may be used to support projects that address financial fraud in a collaborative fashion.
Justice (Office on Violence Against Women)	Enhanced Training and Services to End Violence Against and Abuse of Women Later in Life Program:Requires a partnership of criminal justice agencies, prosecutors, and nonprofits.

Source: GAO analysis of HHS and Justice documents and interviews.

Collaboration on International and Interstate Financial Crimes

AoA's Elder Justice Community Collaborations program offered over 40 $10,000 grants, along with technical assistance and training, from 2007 to 2010 for the purpose of setting up elder justice coalitions. These coalitions, which included members across a broad range of disciplines, were required to create an elder justice strategic plan for their community, including plans for continuation beyond the grant period. This program was the only one we identified that was created specifically for the purpose of setting up new coalitions; other grants either allowed funds to be used for that purpose or required a coalition to be in place to implement the grant-funded initiative.

International Mass Marketing Scam

From 2005 to 2009, about 100 older adults wired or mailed millions of dollars to scam artists working out of "boiler rooms" in a Middle Eastern country, in response to a phone call from "an attorney" claiming they had won a lottery or sweepstakes but had to first pay several thousand dollars in "taxes" or "fees" to receive their winnings. The perpetrators used information individuals had provided on sweepstakes entry forms to target older adults with some savings or assets, in particular. Many of the victims, who ranged in age from 70 to 80, suffered from debilitating conditions including Alzheimer's or some other form of dementia. Once the perpetrators received a payment, they re-contacted victims to inform them that they needed to send more. Victims typically did as they were told, continuing to send tens and even hundreds of thousands of dollars. To lend legitimacy to this elaborate scheme, victims were sent fake documents that appeared to come from the U.S. Internal Revenue Service or another government agency, and received calls from perpetrators impersonating public officials.

In addition to losing their life savings, victims of this scam suffered emotional distress and declining health. The FBI was the lead U.S. investigating agency in this case.

Six suspects pled guilty to conspiracy charges filed by the U.S. Attorney's Office involving wire and mail fraud through telemarketing. Several were sentenced to between 40 and 150 months in prison. Four more have been extradited to the United States and are

Interstate or international mass marketing scams include "grandparent scams," which persuade victims to wire money to bail "grandchildren" out of jail or pay their expenses, and foreign lottery scams that require victims to pay sizeable sums before they can receive their winnings.[55] In 2011, the FBI's Internet Crime Complaint Center[56] received over 300,000 complaints from victims of all ages about online fraud alone, with reported losses of about $485 million.

Local law enforcement authorities in the four states we visited indicated that investigating and prosecuting the growing number of cases involving interstate and international mass marketing fraud, which often target older adults, is particularly difficult for them. For example, coordinating with law enforcement authorities in other jurisdictions is labor intensive,[57] so state and local officials are often unable to pursue these cases themselves. Furthermore, even though various federal agencies have the authority to investigate and prosecute interstate and international scams (see figure 3),[58] local law enforcement officials told us there is not enough information available on whom they should contact when they need to refer a case to the federal level. They indicated that the lines of communication between local and federal agencies tend to be informal, based on whom local law enforcement officers know in a federal agency.

Providing accurate contact information is consistent with Justice's strategic objective for fiscal years 2012-2016 to strengthen its relationships with state and local law enforcement. Justice officials told us they believe that local officials know which federal officials to contact about international and interstate cases, but state and local law enforcement officials told us that it would be helpful to have more specific information. Cases that local officials do not refer to a federal agency due to a lack of correct contact information may not be investigated or prosecuted by either federal or local authorities.

In addition to not knowing whom to contact, state and local law enforcement officials in the four states we reviewed told us that they are concerned that federal agencies do not take enough of the cases that are referred to them. For example, a law enforcement official from California described a case of widespread interstate check fraud, expressing frustration with federal agencies that would not provide any support when he requested it. Federal officials, on the other hand, told us that they cannot take all cases referred to them by state and local law enforcement and that they must prioritize their caseload to make the best use of their limited resources.

Justice and FTC officials said they tend to focus on larger cases in which many victims were affected or a significant amount of money was lost, and Justice's U.S. Attorneys also apply regional priorities, such as the vulnerability (including age) of the victim, when determining which cases to take.

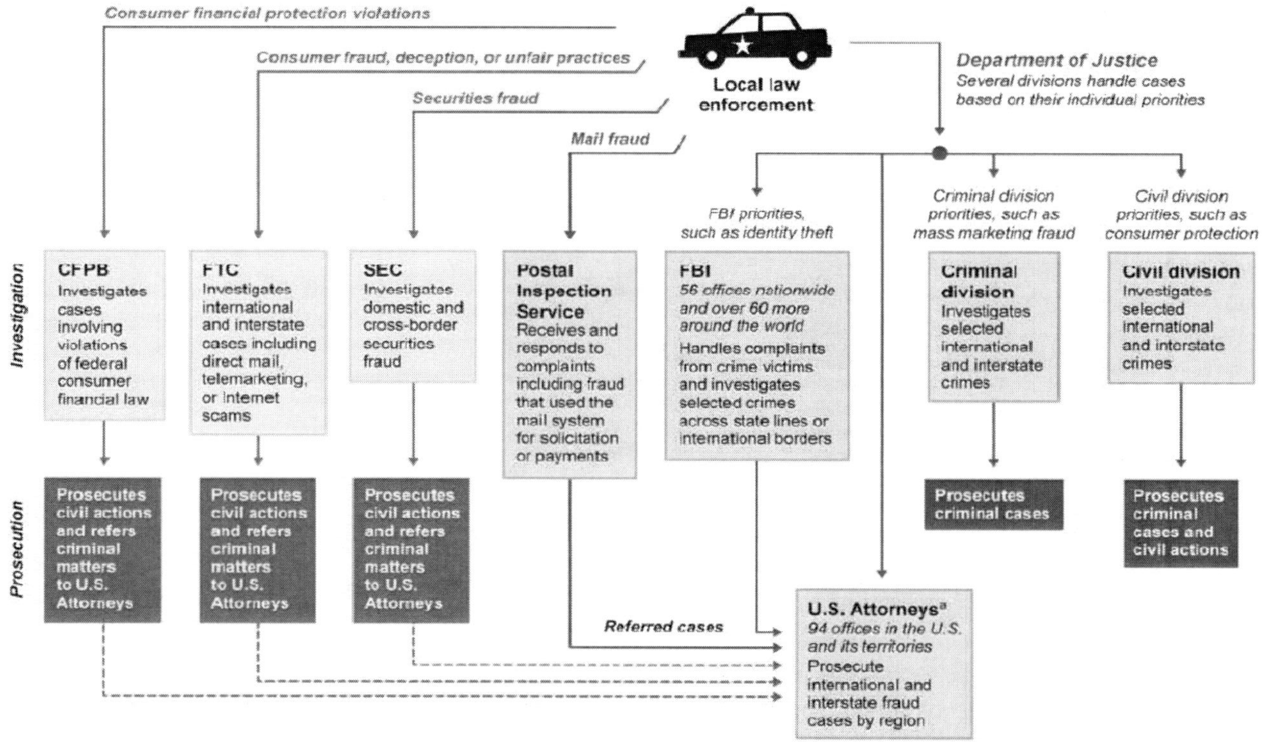

U.S. Attorneys also participate in the investigation of cases, either alone or in cooperation with other agencies.

Figure 3. Federal Agencies' Responsibilities in Combating International and Interstate Financial Crimes.

Even if federal agencies choose not to take a case a state or local agency refers to them, officials told us that consistent referrals of cases by state and local authorities allow them to identify patterns or combine several complaints against the same individual into one case. FTC's Consumer Sentinel Network database (Consumer Sentinel) collects consumer complaint data and aims to be an information-sharing tool to enable state and local law enforcement to become more effective.[59] Justice officials said they encourage individuals and state and local authorities to file a complaint of suspected fraud to either the Consumer Sentinel or the FBI's Internet Crime Complaint Center. However, while some state Attorneys General were familiar with the FTC database, local law enforcement officials we spoke with did not say that they reported cases to it or used its data. One official said he did not find the Consumer Sentinel database useful because law enforcement officials are not familiar with it.

FTC officials explained that while they have made attempts to get state-level offices to contribute to the Consumer Sentinel, barriers such as reservations about data sharing, obsolete technological infrastructure, and severe budgetary cutbacks have kept the numbers of contributors low. When state officials do not contribute to the Consumer Sentinel, the information in the database does not give a national picture of the extent of cross-border scams. As a result of this—in addition to the impact of some law enforcement officials not using the system—it may be more difficult to combat these scams, and officials at all levels may not have the information they need to target their resources appropriately.

Working Cooperatively with Banks

According to state and local officials, banks are important partners in combating elder financial exploitation because they are well-positioned to recognize, report, and provide evidence in these cases. Indeed, frontline bank staff are able to observe elder financial exploitation firsthand. For example, a bank teller who sees an older adult regularly is likely to notice if that individual is accompanied by someone new and seems pressured to withdraw money or if the older adult suddenly begins to wire large sums of money internationally.

There are state efforts and bank policies to help bank employees recognize exploitation. In Illinois, all state-chartered banks are required to train their employees on what constitutes elder financial exploitation.[60] State and local agencies in California and Pennsylvania provide information and training to banks to help them recognize elder financial exploitation. Most of the six banks we spoke with had a policy for periodically training employees on identifying elder financial exploitation. In addition, these banks had a system in place that routinely monitors bank transactions for unusual activity and can help identify exploitation.

Banks may also help report suspected elder financial exploitation to local authorities. Training initiatives, such as Illinois' program, encourage bank employees to report exploitation. Most of the six banks we spoke with had procedures in place for frontline employees to report suspected elder financial exploitation to bank management. Some of these banks also had internal units that are dedicated to receiving staff reports of elder financial exploitation and referring them to the proper authorities.

Notwithstanding such efforts, APS and criminal justice officials told us elder financial exploitation is generally underreported by banks.[61] Despite the training they receive, bank staff may not be aware of the signs of elder financial exploitation or know how to report it. In addition, in five of the six prosecuted cases we reviewed in depth, there were missed opportunities for banks to raise questions about transactions. For example, in one case, bank officials did not take any action in response to repeated withdrawals of large amounts of money that were not typical for that customer. Bank officials said they do report suspected elder financial exploitation, but also emphasized that banks are not law enforcement agencies. Officials said their primary responsibility is to protect customer assets and privacy and ensure customers have access to their funds. In addition, a banking association representative told us that even though federal privacy laws do not prohibit banks from reporting suspected abuse, banks are concerned that they will be held liable if they report suspected exploitation that is not later substantiated.

Three federal agencies—CFPB, AoA, and FinCEN—are positioned to encourage banks to identify and report elder financial exploitation, either due to the agency's mission or via proposed or existing activities. The CFPB is the primary federal consumer protection regulator with respect to a variety of financial institutions, including banks. The Dodd-Frank Act authorizes the CFPB to protect consumers, including older adults, from abusive practices committed in connection with the offering or provision of consumer financial products or services.[62] In a November 2011 congressional testimony, the Assistant Director of CFPB's Office for Older Americans said the agency has a unique opportunity to help enhance, coordinate, and promote efforts of a variety of groups, including financial services providers.[63]

While the federal government generally requires banks to train employees on a variety of issues, such as money laundering, physical bank security, and information security,[64] we could find no similar requirements for banks to train employees to recognize and report elder financial exploitation. However, AoA is considering collaborating with one large national bank on a project to encourage bank training on elder financial exploitation.

Banks are also required to file Suspicious Activity Reports (SAR) with FinCEN to alert them of potentially illegal bank transactions that involve, individually or in the aggregate, at least $5,000, which could include elder financial exploitation.[65] In February 2011, FinCEN issued an advisory to banks that described elder financial exploitation, provided potential indicators of elder financial exploitation, and requested the use of a specific term ("elder financial exploitation") when applicable in SAR narratives related to this activity.[66]

Bank records can help investigators track an older adult's use of funds over time and detect irregularities. APS officials in Pennsylvania told us that although Pennsylvania state law grants APS access to bank records, they are often denied access on the basis of federal privacy laws or the bank's policies. APS officials from California, Illinois, and New York also reported that they are denied access to bank records for the same reasons.[67] As a result, investigators are unable to obtain the information necessary to investigate suspected exploitation, identify perpetrators, stop further exploitation from occurring, or obtain restitution for victims. Bank officials told us the federal government could help clarify bank roles and responsibilities related to privacy and financial exploitation of older adults.[68]

There are two federal laws that generally protect the privacy of consumer banking records: the Right to Financial Privacy Act of 1978 (RFPA)[69] and the Gramm-Leach-Bliley Act.[70] Each establishes standards that banks must meet to safeguard customer banking information. The RFPA generally prohibits financial institutions, including banks, from providing any federal governmental authority with access to copies of information in any customer's records without first providing notice to the customer. Because a government authority is defined in RFPA to include only federal agencies and officials, however, it should not prevent banks from reporting possible financial exploitation of older adults—or providing bank records to—state APS.

The Gramm-Leach-Bliley Act generally prohibits financial institutions, including banks, from disclosing nonpublic personal information to third parties including, but not limited to, federal governmental authorities. Nonetheless, the act has a number of general exceptions permitting disclosure, such as: to protect against or prevent actual or potential fraud, unauthorized transactions, claims, or other liability; consistent with the RFPA, for an investigation on a matter related to public safety; or to comply with a properly authorized civil, criminal, or regulatory investigation, subpoena, or summons by federal, state, or local authorities.

Incomplete Data Hinder Efforts to Combat Elder Financial Exploitation

The NCEA and experts have called for more data on the cost of elder financial exploitation to public programs and for trend data on its extent. According to our analysis, these data could help determine what government resources to allocate and how best to prevent and respond to this problem. According to one Utah official, quantifying the impact of elder financial exploitation in that state helped that state's legislators understand the importance of combating this problem and convinced them to simply decrease, rather than eliminate, state APS funding altogether.[71] However, according to our analysis, no other state has undertaken such a study.

Similarly, data on the extent of elder financial exploitation over time could help state and local APS, as well as law enforcement agencies, assess the effectiveness of their efforts to combat it. The OAA[72] and EJA both require the federal government to take steps to collect and disseminate data on all types of elder abuse,[73] yet the studies federal agencies have funded in this area have produced little data on its extent over time, as we previously reported,[74] or on its cost.

Several federal agencies do collect administrative data on the number of complaints submitted by consumers or criminal cases that sometimes involve elder financial exploitation (see table 5)—data that could help state and local APS and law enforcement authorities determine what resources to allocate and how best to prevent and respond to this problem. Each agency publishes material containing a range of administrative data from its system that is available to the public. FTC, for example, publishes statistics from the Consumer Sentinel on the number and types of complaints, amount of losses, and characteristics of victims.[75]

While the number of reported incidents of elder financial exploitation in each agency's system represents only a portion of all cases that actually occur in a given period and geographic area, the number over time could provide an indication of fluctuations in the extent of certain types of elder financial exploitation.

Table 5. Federal Administrative Data Systems That Collect Incidents of Elder Financial Exploitation

Data System/Agency	Information Collected	Identifies Age of Victim?	Contributors
FTC's Consumer Sentinel Network	Information on consumer complaints, including investment and mass marketing fraud, and identity theft. The FTC adds cases from the FBI's Internet Crime Complaint Center to the Consumer Sentinel.	Optional. Less than half of complaints currently include age.	Some state and local law enforcement agencies, federalagencies, nongovernmental and private entities, and individuals.
FinCEN's SAR Data	Information on suspicious financial transactions, both actual and attempted.	Option to identify suspected elder financial exploitation[a]and age of victim.	Banks and other financial institutions.
FBI's Internet Crime Complaint Center	Complaints about cyber-crime, including online fraud.	Age is a required field.	State and local law enforcement agencies, as wellas individuals.
Justice's National Incident-Based Reporting System	Each single incident of and arrest for 46 crimes collected from state, local, and federal law enforcement agencies that participate in the system.	Age is a required field for individual victims.	State and local law enforcement agencies.
SEC's Tips, Complaints, and Referrals Portal	Complaints about investments or financial professionals.	Information about age is not required.	All sources, including individualinvestors.

Source: GAO analysis of documents provided and interviews granted by FTC, FinCEN, Justice, and SEC.

[a] In 2012, FinCEN released a revised SAR that includes a check box that enables filers to indicate clearly that they are reporting suspected elder financial exploitation. The revised SAR is currently available for use, and will become mandatory at the end of March 2013, according to FinCEN officials.

Data from the Consumer Sentinel could be of particular interest to state and local APS and law enforcement authorities, because over half of the consumer complaints reported to this system involve financial exploitation through fraud. Individual complaints can be directly reported to the Consumer Sentinel by victims or others on their behalf. Cases reported to the FBI Internet Crime Complaint Center and non-governmental organizations, such as the Council of Better Business Bureaus, are also added to the complaints in the Consumer Sentinel. Currently, however, the Consumer Sentinel does not receive any of the complaints reported to any of the law enforcement or consumer protection agencies in 38 states. Moreover, less than half the complaints in the Consumer Sentinel contain the age of the victim because FTC does not require complaints to include this information or other indicators of whether the case involved elder financial exploitation.[76] FTC officials told us the agency does not require complaints to include the age of the victim because of concerns regarding privacy and the potential burden this might place on individual complainants. In contrast, SARs in the FinCEN system will soon all be clearly identified when a filing institution reports suspected elder financial exploitation.

In 2011, we found that state-level APS data could provide useful information on the extent of elder abuse, including elder financial exploitation, over time. We recommended that AoA work with states to develop a nationwide system to collect and compile these data.[77] AoA officials told us they have initiated discussions with states about establishing such a system, but have been unable to develop a comprehensive plan for implementing one due to a lack of funding.

CONCLUSION

Elder financial exploitation is a multi-faceted problem spanning social service, criminal justice and consumer protection systems of government. As a result, combating it is challenging and requires action on the part of not only many state and local agencies, but also multiple agencies at the federal level. Each of the seven federal agencies we reviewed is working to solve this problem in ways that are consistent with its own mission. However, the problem is large and growing. It calls for a more cohesive and deliberate approach governmentwide that, at a minimum, identifies gaps in efforts nationwide, ensures that federal resources are effectively allocated, establishes federal agency responsibilities, and holds agencies accountable for meeting them. The EJCC has recognized that combating elder abuse, including elder financial exploitation, is an effort that requires federal agencies to work together. A clearly articulated national strategy is needed to coordinate and optimize such federal efforts to effectively prevent and respond to elder financial exploitation, and the EJCC can be the vehicle for defining and implementing this strategy. In the current economic climate, state and local APS and law enforcement agencies will find it increasingly difficult to cope with growing numbers of cases without a national strategy attuned to their need for information and guidance on preventing and responding to elder financial exploitation, as well as additional data on its extent and impact.

In addition to working together to build a national strategy to combat elder financial exploitation, there are a number of ways individual federal agencies could better support state and local APS and law enforcement agencies. For example, Justice has identified providing training and resources to combat elder abuse as a strategy to achieve its objectives of preventing and intervening in crimes against vulnerable populations. Without easily accessible information and guidance tailored to the needs of prosecutors nationwide, they may continue, given limited resources, to make such cases a low priority. Similarly, many cases cross jurisdictions and could involve multiple victims or have perpetrators located in other countries. These cases may not be investigated or prosecuted unless state and local law enforcement have better information on the process for contacting the federal government regarding these cases or the ways in which the federal government could provide support.

Without information to correct banks' misconceptions about the impact of federal privacy laws on their ability to release bank records, APS and law enforcement agencies will continue to find it difficult to obtain the information they need from banks to investigate suspected cases of elder financial exploitation. Moreover, without educating bank employees nationwide on how to identify and report suspected elder financial exploitation, many cases will continue to go unreported, uninvestigated, and unprosecuted. The CPFB is positioned to provide additional information to banks, as part of the agency's consumer protection regulatory function and dedication to protecting the financial health of older Americans.

Finally, to fulfill its mission of protecting consumers against unfair, deceptive, or fraudulent practices, the FTC established the Consumer Sentinel Network database to enhance information-sharing and support law enforcement at all levels. The Consumer Sentinel could serve as a valuable source of data on the extent of some types of elder financial exploitation nationwide and as an important resource for law enforcement authorities as they identify, investigate, and prosecute cases. The Consumer Sentinel's usefulness in this area, however, will continue to be limited until the number of contributors to it is increased and complaints are required to include the age of the victim or other indicators of whether the case involved elder financial exploitation. In the absence of the latter, it is difficult to determine the number of financial exploitation complaints that involve older adults, which in turn makes any Consumer Sentinel data contributed less useful to state and local APS and law enforcement agencies.

RECOMMENDATIONS FOR EXECUTIVE ACTION

To coordinate and optimize federal efforts to prevent and respond to elder financial exploitation, we recommend the Secretary of HHS, as chairman of the Elder Justice Coordinating Council, direct the Council to develop a written national strategy for combating this problem. This strategy should include a clear statement of its purpose and goals and indicate the roles and responsibilities particular federal agencies should have in implementing it. The strategy could address, among other things, the need to

- identify and disseminate promising practices and other information nationwide that can be used by state and local agencies to prevent exploitation, educate the public, and help state and local agencies collaborate, investigate, and prosecute elder financial exploitation;
- ensure coordination of public awareness activities across federal agencies; and
- collect and disseminate better data nationwide to inform federal, state, and local decisions regarding prevention of and response to elder financial exploitation.

To develop expertise among prosecutors and other criminal justice officials, we recommend the Attorney General establish timeframes for and take the steps necessary to launch the elder justice prosecution website that Justice has begun to construct.

To facilitate investigation and prosecution of interstate and international elder financial exploitation, we recommend the Attorney General conduct outreach to state and local law enforcement agencies to clarify the process for contacting the federal government regarding these cases and the ways in which the federal government could provide support. To encourage banks to identify and report suspected elder financial exploitation and to facilitate release of bank records to APS and law enforcement authorities for investigating this activity, we recommend the Director of the Consumer Financial Protection Bureau

- develop a plan to educate banks nationwide on how to identify and report possible elder financial exploitation; and
- develop and disseminate information for banks on the circumstances under which they are permitted, under federal privacy laws, to release relevant bank records to law enforcement and APS agencies.

To increase the usefulness of data from the Consumer Sentinel Network database for federal, state, and local investigation and prosecution of elder financial exploitation, we recommend the Chairman of the Federal Trade Commission:

- take additional steps to encourage more state and local law enforcement authorities nationwide to report to the Consumer Sentinel relevant individual complaints they receive of elder financial exploitation and to encourage and enable these authorities to query the system; and
- study the feasibility of requiring that all complaints to the Consumer Sentinel include either the victim's age or an indication of whether the complaint involves elder financial exploitation

RESPONSE TO AGENCY COMMENTS

We provided a draft of this report to the seven federal agencies that we reviewed for their comments. CFPB concurred with our recommendations and agreed that a collaborative and coordinated effort by federal agencies can help optimize strategies to combat elder financial. CFPB further noted that financial institutions can play a key role in preventing and detecting elder financial exploitation, and that CFPB is collecting information on financial institution training programs and considering how best to help institutions that request this information. HHS indicated in its general comments that our recommendations are consistent with what it heard during the inaugural meeting of the EJCC, and added that it looks forward to working with Congress to continue implementing the EJA.

In an e-mailed response, FTC's Bureau of Consumer Protection noted that the Consumer Sentinel database provides law enforcement with access to millions of consumer complaints. FTC added that the database has no required fields, and expressed its belief that if consumers were required to provide detailed personal information as a condition to filing a complaint, they might refuse to do so, thereby decreasing the overall effectiveness of the system. FTC explained that almost 48 percent of all fraud complaints in 2011 included the voluntary submission of age, and that nearly half of its non-individual data contributors do not submit age information in the data they provide to FTC. Given the potential for the Consumer Sentinel database to support and enhance state and local law enforcement agencies' response to elder financial exploitation, particularly interstate and international cases, we continue to believe that FTC should study the feasibility of requiring that all complaints to the Consumer Sentinel database include the victim's age or another indicator of whether the complaint involves elder financial exploitation. In doing so, FTC can examine different options, including the use of a check box similar to the one that FinCEN has included in its SARs.

Kay E. Brown, Director
Education, Workforce, and Income Security Issues

APPENDIX I: ADMINISTRATION ON AGING (HHS)[1]

Mission

To develop a comprehensive, coordinated, and cost-effective system of home- and community-based services that helps elderly individuals maintain their health and independence.

How Agency Prioritizes Elder Financial Exploitation

Strategic goal of ensuring the rights of older people and preventing their abuse, neglect, and exploitation.

Agency's Role in Combating Elder Financial Exploitation

The Older Americans Act Amendments of 1965 calls for AoA to develop objectives, priorities, policy, and a long-term plan for facilitating the development of a coordinated, multidisciplinary elder justice system in the United States

The Elder Justice Act of 2009 (EJA) calls for HHS to, among other things:

- collect and disseminate data related to exploitation,
- conduct research on and develop information on best practices for Adult Protective Services (APS),
- provide technical assistance to APS, and
- establish centers to conduct research, develop expertise, and improve law enforcement's ability to combat elder financial exploitation

Contact Information

Call: (202) 619-0724
Email: aoainfo@aoa.hhs.gov

Source: GAO analysis of AoA documents and interviews.

Relevant Agency Divisions

Assistant Secretary for Aging: Assists the Secretary with activities that address challenges and opportunities for older adults

Office of Elder Rights: Administers the provisions of the Older Americans Act related to elder abuse prevention

Selected Activities

- Funds and oversees the National Center for Elder Abuse (NCEA; www.ncea.aoa.gov), a national resource center dedicated to preventing elder abuse
- Funded the National Adult Protective Services Resource Center, which provides information and technical assistance to APS officials
- Provides formula grants to State Units on Aging in each state to prevent elder abuse
- Provides funds to local legal services providers, which may use the funds to assist elder financial exploitation victims

- AoA's Model Approaches to Statewide Legal Assistance Systems program funds demonstration grants, which aim to strengthen states' legal services networks, may be used to support projects that address elder financial exploitation

Coordination with Other Agencies

- Works with state aging agencies to help them develop statewide plans to combat elder abuse
- Through NCEA, partnered with Treasury on its Go Direct financial literacy campaign
- Partnered with Treasury and the Financial Services Roundtable on a toolkit for training financial institutions on elder financial exploitation
- Worked with the SEC on several Seniors Summits that brought agencies together to discuss elder financial exploitation
- Chairs the Elder Justice Coordinating Council, a collaborative body of federal agencies created under the EJA to recommend federal policies to combat elder abuse and ways federal agencies should coordinate to implement these policies.
- Co-leads an informal interagency workgroup that helps facilitate federal elder justice activities.

APPENDIX II: CONSUMER FINANCIAL PROTECTION BUREAU (CFPB)

Mission

To implement and enforce federal consumer financial law consistently for the purpose of ensuring that all consumers have access to markets for consumer financial products and services and that markets for consumer financial products and services are fair, transparent, and competitive

How agency prioritizes elder financial exploitation

Agency's organizing statute requires emphasis on older Americans and protecting them from financial exploitation

Agency's role in combating elder financial exploitation

Leadership: Office for Older Americans is the first federal office dedicated to the financial health of older Americans

Information dissemination: Provides information to consumers and to others who assist them in combating elder financial exploitation

Supervision and Enforcement: Supervises certain banks and nonbanks and brings enforcement actions when appropriate

Rulemaking: Issues rules, orders, and guidance

Contact information

Call: (855) 411-2372

General Information: www.consumerfinance.gov

Source: GAO analysis of CFPB documents and interviews.

Organization

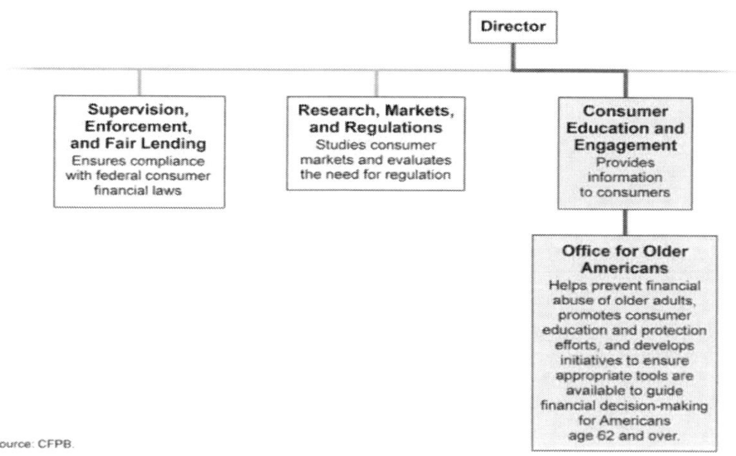

Source: CFPB.

Selected Activities

- Posts information for older adults on website
- Conducts research on issues affecting older Americans, such as reverse mortgages, financial advisors and their credentials, and fiduciaries

- Gathering information from the public on elder financial exploitation to learn more about the ways in which older adults are financially exploited and best practices for elder financial management. CFPB expects to share its results in 2013.

Coordination with Other Agencies

- Member of the Elder Justice Coordinating Council
- Member of Financial Fraud Enforcement Task Force, which brings numerous federal agencies together to prevent, investigate, and prosecute financial crime
- Works with AoA, Justice, Department of Labor, and SEC on various projects related to protecting older Americans

APPENDIX III: FEDERAL TRADE COMMISSION (FTC)

Mission

To prevent business practices that are anticompetitive, deceptive, or unfair to consumers; to enhance informed consumer choice and public understanding of the competitive process; and to accomplish this without unduly burdening legitimate business activity

How agency prioritizes elder financial exploitation

FTC identifies older adults as a target population for its consumer education efforts. Elder financial exploitation is included as part of the Bureau of Consumer Protection's responsibility to protect all consumers.

Agency's role in combating elder financial exploitation

Legal action: Investigates and prosecutes large-scale fraud cases
Information dissemination: Provides educational materials to consumers

Data collection: FTC's Consumer Sentinel database stores individual fraud complaints; other federal, state, and local agencies use and submit information to the database

Contact information
1-877-FTC-HELP (1-877-382-4357)
General information: www.ftc.gov
To submit a complaint online: www.ftccomplaintassistant.gov/

Source: GAO analysis of FTC documents and interviews.

Relevant Agency Divisions

Bureau of Consumer Protection: Works to protect consumers against unfair, deceptive, or fraudulent practices in the marketplace. The Bureau conducts investigations, sues companies and people who violate the law, develops rules to protect consumers, and educates consumers and businesses about their rights and responsibilities. The Bureau also collects complaints about consumer fraud and identity theft and makes them available to law enforcement agencies across the country.

- The Divisions of Advertising Practices, Enforcement, Financial Practices, Marketing Practices, and Privacy and Identity Protection, and FTC Regional Offices are involved to some extent in the Bureau's elder financial exploitation activities.
- The Division of Consumer and Business Education's mission is to give consumers the tools they need to make informed decisions and to give businesses the tools they need to comply with law. The Division produces, promotes, and disseminates information that is timely, targeted, objective, actionable, and in plain language.

Selected Activities

- The Enforcement Division, as part of its overall mission, has dedicated resources to investigating misrepresentations aimed at the "oldest old" and their caretakers. In 2012, the Division settled two administrative cases with companies that misrepresented the services they provide when referring seniors to long-term care facilities.
- In April 2012, the Division of Privacy and Identity Protection gathered information on the types of senior identity theft, how it happens, and possible solutions.

- FTC actively prosecutes fraudulent telemarketers, online and direct mail merchants engaged in a wide variety of deceptive scams.

Coordination with Other Agencies

- Member of Financial Fraud Enforcement Task Force, which brings numerous federal agencies together to prevent, investigate, and prosecute financial crime
- May work with international, federal, state, and local law enforcement officials to investigate cases and bring enforcement actions against scammers
- Hosts Common Ground Conferences that bring federal, state, local agencies and non-profit organizations together to share information on scams

APPENDIX IV: FINANCIAL CRIMES ENFORCEMENT NETWORK (FINCEN)

Mission

To enhance the integrity of financial systems by facilitating the detection and deterrence of financial crime

How agency prioritizes elder financial exploitation

FinCEN does not specifically identify protecting older adults in its agency priorities; however, it recently released a new Suspicious Activity Report form that enables financial institutions specifically to identify suspected elder financial exploitation

Agency's role in combating elder financial exploitation

Law enforcement: FinCEN supports financial criminal investigations, most often those involving money laundering

Data collection: FinCEN aggregates data reported by financial institutions on suspicious activity reports, including reports of suspected elder financial exploitation

Rulemaking: FinCEN can issue rules and regulations implementing the Bank Secrecy Act of 1970[a] (anti-money laundering), as amended by the USA PATRIOT Act[b]

Contact information
Regulatory Helpline : (800) 949-2732
General information: http://www.fincen.gov
Source: GAO analysis of FinCEN documents and interviews.

Organization

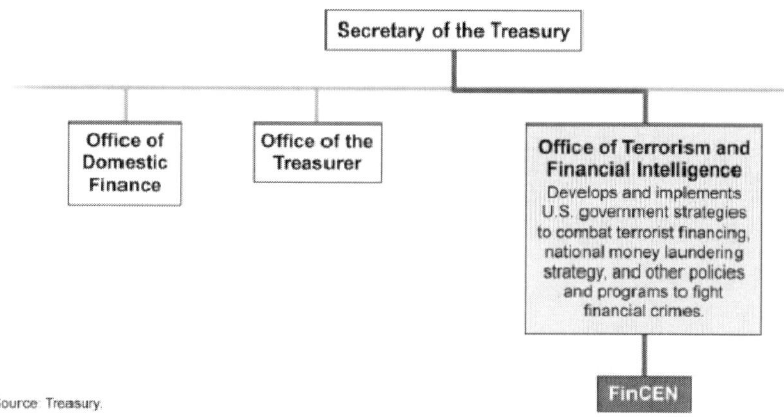

Source: Treasury.

Selected Activities

- Provides analytical support to law enforcement investigations and access to Suspicious Activity Reports collected from financial institutions under the Bank Secrecy Act of 1970
- Regulates financial institutions, requiring them to have anti-money laundering programs and to report suspicious activity, including elder financial exploitation
- Issued advisory to financial institutions with information about how to identify and report elder financial exploitation

Coordination with Other Agencies

- Member of Financial Fraud Enforcement Task Force, which brings numerous federal agencies together to prevent, investigate, and prosecute financial crime

[a] Pub. L. No. 91-508, 84 Stat. 1114 (codified as amended at 12 U.S.C. §§ 1829(b), 1951-1959; 31 U.S.C. §§ 5311-5330).

[b] The Uniting and Strengthening America by Providing Appropriate Tools Required to Intercept and Obstruct Terrorism (USA PATRIOT ACT) Act of 2001, Pub. L. No. 107-56, 115 Stat 272 (2001). We refer to this act as the USA PATRIOT Act.

APPENDIX V: DEPARTMENT OF JUSTICE

Mission

To enforce the law and defend the interests of the United States according to the law; to ensure public safety against threats foreign and domestic; to provide federal leadership in preventing and controlling crime; to seek just punishment for those guilty of unlawful behavior; and to ensure fair and impartial administration of justice for all Americans

How agency prioritizes elder financial exploitation

Priority goal of protecting vulnerable populations, including the elderly

Agency's role in combating elder financial exploitation

Assistance to victims: Provided as part of the Victims of Crime Act Crime Victims Fund and Violence Against Women Act of 1994, as amended

Research, technical assistance, and training: Funds research in the field of elder abuse and technical assistance and training to those in the field

Law enforcement: Investigates fraud crimes and makes arrests

Legal action: Prosecutes fraud cases

Contact information

Main number: 202-514-2000; On the web: www.justice.gov

Source: GAO analysis of Justice documents and interviews.

Organization

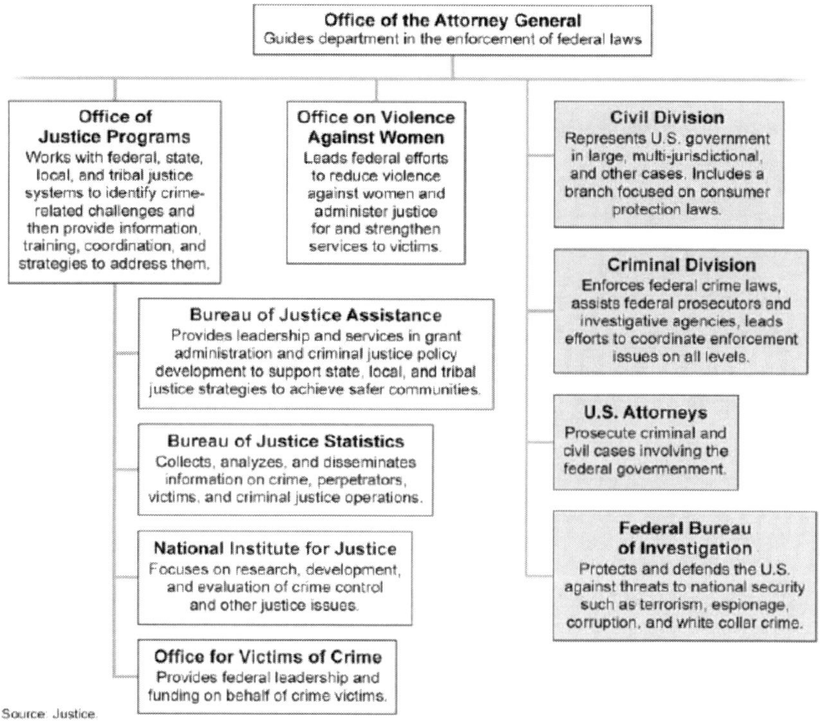

Source: Justice.

Selected Activities

- Prosecutes perpetrators of elder financial exploitation
- Conducts public awareness activities on elder financial exploitation
- Office on Violence Against Women and Office for Victims of Crime both provide grants for training that includes elder financial exploitation

- Bureau of Justice Statistics and National Institute of Justice both fund or conduct studies on elder financial exploitation
- See FBI and U.S. Attorney pages for details on those agencies

Coordination with Other Agencies

- Mandated member of Elder Justice Coordinating Council
- Member of Elder Justice Working Group
- Coordinates the Financial Fraud Enforcement Task Force, which brings numerous federal agencies together to prevent, investigate, and prosecute financial crime

Appendix VI: Federal Bureau of Investigation (FBI)

Mission

To protect and defend the United States against terrorist and foreign intelligence threats, to uphold and enforce the criminal laws of the United States; and to provide leadership and criminal justice services to federal, state, municipal, and international agencies and partners

How agency prioritizes elder financial exploitation

Priority goal of combating financial/white collar crime.
Mass marketing fraud, which may include elder financial exploitation, ranks fourth among the FBI's financial crime priorities

Agency's role in combating elder financial exploitation

Law enforcement: Investigates fraud crimes and makes arrests

Contact information
Main number: 202-324-3000;
On the web: www.fbi.gov
To find your field office: www.fbi.gov/contact-us/field

Source: GAO analysis of FBI documents and interviews.

Organization

56 field offices located in major metropolitan areas and in Puerto Rico, as well as legal attaches in U.S. embassies around the world

Selected Activities

- Responds to complaints from victims of crime
- Investigates selected cases of potential elder financial exploitation.
- Internet Crime Complaint Center receives complaints about internet-related crime and shares them with the Federal Trade Commission (FTC) Consumer Sentinel Network database and federal, state, and local law enforcement offices as appropriate
- Conducts outreach about elder financial exploitation to local entities such as nursing homes and financial institutions

Coordination with Other Agencies

- Works with local U.S. Attorneys' offices to make determinations about whether to open or continue investigations of potential elder financial exploitation cases
- Works with other federal and state agencies, such as the U.S. Postal Inspection Service, to conduct investigations
- May work jointly with foreign law enforcement agencies to investigate international mass marketing fraud cases
- Coordinates with the National White Collar Crime Center to run the Internet Crime Complaint Center (see above)
- Maintains Memorandum of Understanding with the FTC to get access to FTC's Consumer Sentinel Network database
- Participates in regional task forces on financial crime
- Member of Financial Fraud Enforcement Task Force, which brings numerous federal agencies together to prevent, investigate, and prosecute financial crime

Appendix VII: U.S. Attorneys

Mission

As the nation's principal litigators, U.S. Attorneys prosecute criminal cases brought by the federal government; prosecute and defend civil cases in which the United States is a party; and collect certain debts owed to the federal government

How agency prioritizes elder financial exploitation

Each U.S. Attorney exercises wide discretion in determining which cases to pursue to best use the office's resources to further the priorities and needs of their jurisdiction. Offices may prioritize investment and securities fraud

Agency's role in combating elder financial exploitation

Law enforcement: Investigates fraud crimes and makes arrests
Legal action: Prosecutes fraud cases

Contact information
On the web: www.justice.gov/usao
To find your field office: http://www.justice.gov/usao/about/offices.html

Source: GAO analysis of Justice documents and interviews.

Organization

94 offices across the country and in U.S. territories

Selected Activities

- Prosecutes perpetrators of elder financial exploitation
- Provides assistance to elder financial exploitation victims

Coordination with Other Agencies

- May receive cases from other federal agencies, such as the FBI, the Postal Inspectors, and the SEC, as well as from state and local agencies
- May pursue cases in conjunction with partner agencies
- Participates in regional task forces on financial crime
- Member of the Financial Fraud Enforcement Task Force, which brings numerous federal agencies together to prevent, investigate, and prosecute financial crime

APPENDIX VIII: U.S. POSTAL INSPECTION SERVICE

Mission

To support and protect the U.S. Postal Service and its employees, infrastructure, and customers; enforce the laws that defend the nation's mail system from illegal or dangerous use; and ensure public trust in the mail

How agency prioritizes elder financial exploitation

The Postal Inspection Service does not specifically identify protecting older adults in its agency priorities; however, older adults are often victimized in the mail fraud schemes it investigates

Agency's role in combating elder financial exploitation

Law enforcement: Investigates mail fraud crimes and makes arrests and has administrative authority to shut down addresses used for fraud

Information dissemination: Provides information to the public about mail fraud

Data collection: Tracks data on its cases, mines data for trends, and shares this data with FTC's Consumer Sentinel Network database

Contact information

Main number: 1-877-876-2445;

On the web: postalinspectors.uspis.gov

Source: GAO analysis of agency documents and interviews.

Organization

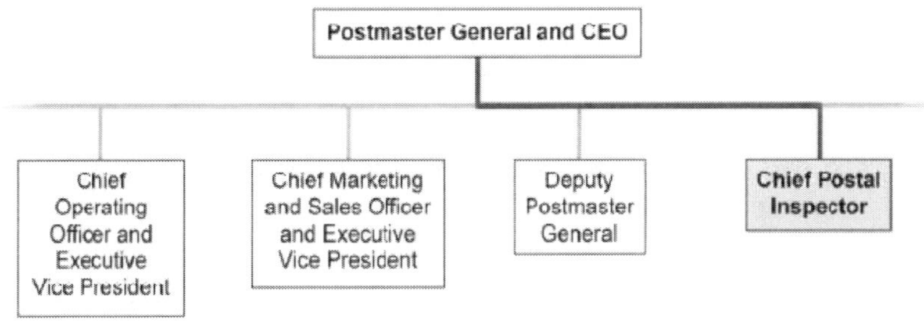

Source: U.S. Postal Service.

Selected Activities

- 2010 mass mailing to every U.S. household on fraud, including elder financial exploitation
- Community presentations about scams during National Consumer Protection Week
- Participates in community discussions about mail fraud, such as an AARP Town Hall meeting and a panel discussion hosted by Stanford Research Center on the Prevention of Financial Fraud
- Plans to have a campaign in 2013 on preventing fraudulent lottery schemes, focusing on older adults

Coordination with Other Agencies

- Member of the Elder Justice Coordinating Council
- Member of the Financial Fraud Enforcement Task Force, which brings numerous federal agencies together to prevent, investigate, and prosecute financial crime
- Collaborates with Canadian and Jamaican criminal justice systems on international fraud
- Collaborates with FTC on National Consumer Protection Week

Appendix IX: Securities and Exchange Commission (SEC)

Mission

To protect investors; maintain fair, orderly, and efficient markets; and facilitate capital formation

How agency prioritizes elder financial exploitation

SEC does not specifically identify elder financial exploitation as a priority, but it does identify older adults as a target population for its investor education, enforcement, and industry-compliance related efforts

Agency's role in combating elder financial exploitation

Supervision of investment professionals: Conducts exams and inspections of investment professionals, such as broker-dealers, investment companies, and investment advisors

Legal action: Conducts investigations and prosecutes violations of the federal securities laws

Information dissemination: Provides educational materials to investors

Rulemaking: Establishes rules on matters affecting the operations of securities markets

Contact information

Investor Information Service: 1-800-SEC-0330
www.sec.gov
www.investor.gov

Source: GAO analysis of SEC documents and interviews.

Relevant Agency Divisions

Office of Investor Education and Advocacy: Carries out SEC's investor education program; responds to questions and complaints from members of the public; and reviews agency rulemaking from the perspective of the individual investor

Division of Enforcement: Conducts investigations into possible violations of the federal securities laws, and prosecutes cases in civil suits in the federal courts, and in administrative proceedings before an administrative law judge

Office of Compliance Inspections and Examinations: Administers the SEC's nationwide examination and inspection program and conducts inspections to foster compliance with securities laws and to detect violations of the laws

Division of Trading and Markets: Assists the Commission in executing its responsibility for maintaining fair, orderly, and efficient markets, including day-to-day oversight of major securities market participants

Selected Activities

- Published A Guide for Seniors: Protect Yourself Against Investment Fraud
- Produced reports on free lunch seminars and promising practices that businesses can undertake to prevent and detect fraud against older adults
- Maintains a website that allows investors are able to research investment advisor firms, and provides a link to a similar website for brokers on the Financial Industry Regulatory Authority's (FINRA) website
- Issues approximately 25 investor alerts and bulletins per year
- Works with FINRA, AARP, and state securities regulators on the Outsmarting Investment Fraud campaign, which is designed to reduce investment fraud among older adults

Coordination with Other Agencies

- Member of Financial Fraud Enforcement Task Force, which brings numerous federal agencies together to prevent, investigate, and prosecute financial crime
- Participates in the multi-agency Financial Literacy and Education Commission, which coordinates federal financial education efforts and developed a national strategy for financial literacy

Appendix X: Examples of State and Local Activities to Prevent and Respond to Elder Financial Exploitation

State	Efforts to Prevent Exploitation by Financial Services Providers, Power-of-Attorney Agents, and Paid in-Home Caregivers	Efforts to Educate and Inform Older Adults and the General Public	Efforts to Provide Information to and Enhance Expertise for Professionals Responding to Exploitation	Efforts to Foster Collaboration among Institutions Responding to Exploitation
California	Napa County •Caregiver Ordinance – all in-home caregivers must submit to and pass a background check and obtain a permit to provide services State Law •Mandatory elder abuse reporting for health care professionals, social workers, nursing home workers, and employees of banks and credit unions •Discretionary background checks for paid in-home caregivers Department of Corporations	San Bernardino County APS •Scam blasts are sent to senior centers and law enforcement agencies to alert older adults of potential scams. •"It's not your fault" publication — campaign to reduce elder financial exploitation stigma among older adults San Joaquin District Attorneys Offices Communities Against Senior Exploitation—representatives from the District Attorney's office provide examples of financial fraud and tips for personal safety and protecting personal information San Francisco District Attorney's Office	Institute on Aging •Houses the San Francisco Elder Abuse Forensic Center, which works to improve coordination among those responding to elder abuse cases; assists victims; and educates professionals and the general public on preventing, reporting, and stopping elder abuse San Bernardino County APS •Shift change briefings and pocket guide to elder abuse penal codes for local law enforcement	San Francisco Elder Financial Abuse Collaboration •Participants from across local government and the private sector. Goal is to conduct innovative and comprehensive research and to bring stakeholders together to advocate for improved responses to elder financial abuse. San Francisco

State	Efforts to Prevent Exploitation by Financial Services Providers, Power-of-Attorney Agents, and Paid in-Home Caregivers	Efforts to Educate and Inform Older Adults and the General Public	Efforts to Provide Information to and Enhance Expertise for Professionals Responding to Exploitation	Efforts to Foster Collaboration among Institutions Responding to Exploitation
	•Seniors Against Investment Fraud—older adults are able to check the licensing status of financial services professionals	•"Elder Financial Abuse the Invisible Crime" —outreach/public awareness campaign with posters in different languages urging individuals to report suspected elder financial abuse to APS Department of Corporations •Seniors Against Investment Fraud—alerts and educates Californians over the age of 50 about financial and investment fraud, common scams, and unscrupulous sales practices that specifically target seniors	Center of Excellence on Elder Abuse and Neglect at UC Irvine •Central source of technical assistance, multidisciplinary training, research, and policy issues in CA and nationally Stanford Center for Longevity •Conducts research on financial fraud and older adults •Created a financial fraud research center In collaboration with the Financial Industry Regulatory Authority California District Attorneys Association	•Multidisciplinary Teams —representatives from the fields of aging, civil law, adult protective services, mental health,social work, law enforcement, and other disciplines meet to review complex abuse cases and to learn about service resources and intervention techniques. San Bernardino County •Multidisciplinary Teams—a variety of groups exist, and they discuss issues ranging from those specific to the District Attorney population to limited capacity. Teams also work on training and discuss individual cases. State Law

(Continued)

State	Efforts to Prevent Exploitation by Financial Services Providers, Power-of-Attorney Agents, and Paid in-Home Caregivers	Efforts to Educate and Inform Older Adults and the General Public	Efforts to Provide Information to and Enhance Expertise for Professionals Responding to Exploitation	Efforts to Foster Collaboration among Institutions Responding to Exploitation
				•CA Financial Abuse Reporting Act—employees of banks and credit unions are required to report suspected financial elder abuse to APS or law enforcement authorities
		Department of Financial Institutions •Website: provides information for consumers on preventing and reporting elder financial exploitation,as well as information for banks on reporting requirements	•Provides training for police investigators San Francisco District Attorney •Provides training for CA mandated reporters Elder Financial Protection Network •Events and training for financial professionals	Financial Elder Abuse Roundtable •Consists of Departments of Corporations, Insurance, Attorney General, and Aging. The roundtable hears from local members about issues that are ofconcern and determines how the state might help.

State	Efforts to Prevent Exploitation by Financial Services Providers, Power-of-Attorney Agents, and Paid in-Home Caregivers	Efforts to Educate and Inform Older Adults and the General Public	Efforts to Provide Information to and Enhance Expertise for Professionals Responding to Exploitation	Efforts to Foster Collaboration among Institutions Responding to Exploitation
Illinois	Department on Aging •Volunteer Money Management Program —a protective service for limited income seniors who need help managing their finances State Law •Mandatory elder abuse reporting for social services and health care professionals •Power-of-attorney law enhanced to create liability for the agent in cases of abuse. If an agent violates the law, they will be required to repay what was stolen. •Mandatory background checks for paid in-home caregivers	Department on Aging •"Be a Savvy Senior" —publications designed to raise older adults' awareness of financial exploitation and to teach them to look for the warning signs Attorney General •Fraud alerts —information on the most common scams perpetrated against seniors •"When in Doubt, Check it Out"—consumer fraud hotline to learn of any complaints filed against a company before doing business with them •"Every Cent Counts" —tips for protecting finances of senior citizens •"Just Hang Up" —to warn seniors about telephone scams Cook County Sheriff's Department •Senior Law Enforcement Academy —trains older adults on crime prevention	Department on Aging •B*SAFE program to train bank personnel on how to prevent, detect, and report financial exploitation •"Protocol for Law Enforcement: Responding to Victims of Elder Abuse, Neglect, and Exploitation" - provides model guidelines and investigation procedures for law enforcement responding to elder abuse. Protocol was created in collaboration with the Illinois Family Violence Coordinating Councils •"Reporting Elder Abuse: What Professionals Need to Know" —pamphlet to raise awareness about elder abuse and reporting requirements Attorney General	Department on Aging •Multidisciplinary Teams—representatives from law enforcement, medical, legal, clergy, financial, and mental health sectors consult on complex cases, support case workers, and improve networking among group members Suburban Elder Justice Coalition •Led by AgeOptions, suburban Chicago AAA,the coalition works to improve coordination and cooperation between elder abuse provider agencies and law enforcement. Statewide

(Continued)

State	Efforts to Prevent Exploitation by Financial Services Providers, Power-of-Attorney Agents, and Paid in-Home Caregivers	Efforts to Educate and Inform Older Adults and the General Public	Efforts to Provide Information to and Enhance Expertise for Professionals Responding to Exploitation	Efforts to Foster Collaboration among Institutions Responding to Exploitation
			•Elderly Service Officer Program—40 hours of elder abuse training for law enforcement officers Department of Financial and Professional Regulation and Department on Aging •Training for state-chartered bank employees—a training was developed to identify the indicators of financial exploitation, as well as how to report. Compliance will be checked for during bank examinations.	•TRIAD programs—law enforcement officials, as well as senior community advocates and other community activists. TRIAD activities help implement crime prevention, education and volunteer programsfor older citizens.
New York	NY APS •Financial management —APS receives the older adult's monthly income, pays their bills, and provides money to the older adult for incidentals		NY State Office of Children and Family Services, Bureau of Adult Services	NYC Elder Abuse Center

State	Efforts to Prevent Exploitation by Financial Services Providers, Power-of-Attorney Agents, and Paid in-Home Caregivers	Efforts to Educate and Inform Older Adults and the General Public	Efforts to Provide Information to and Enhance Expertise for Professionals Responding to Exploitation	Efforts to Foster Collaboration among Institutions Responding to Exploitation
	•Power-of-attorney controls—APS can require an accounting of funds from older adult's power-of-attorney agent Brookdale Center for Healthy Aging and Longevity at Hunter College •Daily Money Management Services —helps older adults make financial decisions or make financial decisions on behalf of older adults who are no longer able	NYC Department for Aging •"It's my Money" game created a tool —in collaboration with the Department of Consumer Affairs—that can be used to help older adults avoid financial fraud and scams •Study of prevalence of elder abuse in NY state, in conjunction with LifeSpan and Weill Cornell Medical college Attorney General •"Smart Seniors" publication —a guide for older adults to help guard against scams and prevent elder abuse	•Training on investigating financial exploitation for protective services caseworkers Weill Cornell Medical College Division of Geriatrics and Gerontology •Project on Elder Abuse and Neglect—conducts research and provides training on elder abuse, including financial exploitation Brookdale Center for Healthy Aging and Longevity at Hunter College •Primary trainer of APS workers in NY state	•Goal is to improve professional, organizational and system responses to elder abuse, neglect and exploitation through collaboration and coordination among agencies •Multidisciplinary Teams—representatives from thehealth, mental health, public safety, legal, victim assistance, and social services sectors review, discuss, and coordinate cases of elder abuse; identify problems that can be brought to the attention of others for strategizing and intervention; and identify research needs
	State Law •Revised Power-of-attorney form	NYPD •Community outreach at senior centers		NYC Elder Abuse Network

(Continued)

State	Efforts to Prevent Exploitation by Financial Services Providers, Power-of-Attorney Agents, and Paid in-Home Caregivers	Efforts to Educate and Inform Older Adults and the General Public	Efforts to Provide Information to and Enhance Expertise for Professionals Responding to Exploitation	Efforts to Foster Collaboration among Institutions Responding to Exploitation
	•Mandatory background checks for paid in-home caregivers	NYC Department of Consumer Affairs •"Be a Savvy Senior" —guide for older adults		•Brings police, district attorneys' offices, social service agencies,and others together to discuss legislation, policy, research, and program planning Weinberg Center for Elder Abuse Prevention •Emergency shelter for victims of elder abuse District Attorney's Offices •Elder Abuse or Financial Crimes units with staff working specifically on elder financial exploitation

State	Efforts to Prevent Exploitation by Financial Services Providers, Power-of-Attorney Agents, and Paid in-Home Caregivers	Efforts to Educate and Inform Older Adults and the General Public	Efforts to Provide Information to and Enhance Expertise for Professionals Responding to Exploitation	Efforts to Foster Collaboration among Institutions Responding to Exploitation
Pennsylvania	State Law •Mandatory reporting for healthcare professionals •Mandatory background checks for paid in-home caregivers PA Securities Commission •Investor alerts – a collection of tips, techniques, and advisories for investors	Attorney General •Senior Consumer Reference Guide —information on how to avoid scams and fraud •Senior Crime Prevention University — outreach program to make older adults aware of common scams, to teach them how to avoid becoming a victim, and to know whom to alert when they are concerned about their safety and well-being •"Safe Seniors" Pamphlet — information for older adults on how to protect themselves from abuse, including financial exploitation •Toll-free senior help line	Institute on Protective Services at Temple University •Staff at the Institute, including a financial accountant, provide investigative assistance to APS and law enforcement for elder financial exploitation cases •Develops curriculum and provides training to APS Philadelphia Corporation for the Aging •Staff member who only works on financial exploitation cases •Training to bank employees, local prosecutors, and other professionals on elder financial exploitation	Philadelphia Financial Exploitation Task Force •Collaboration between APS, law enforcement, and private sector, with the goal of promoting awareness and prevention campaigns, delivering training, and increasing their joint capacity to conduct focused investigations and effectively prosecute cases Statewide •Elder Abuse Task Forces - task forces review elder abuse cases on a regular basis and membership may include APS, law enforcement, judges, clergy, bankers, healthcare providers, or others

(Continued)

State	Efforts to Prevent Exploitation by Financial Services Providers, Power-of-Attorney Agents, and Paid in-Home Caregivers	Efforts to Educate and Inform Older Adults and the General Public	Efforts to Provide Information to and Enhance Expertise for Professionals Responding to Exploitation	Efforts to Foster Collaboration among Institutions Responding to Exploitation
		Philadelphia Police Department •Outreach at senior centers PA Securities Commission •Elder Investment Fraud and Financial Exploitation Prevention Program (EIFFE)—educates medical professionals about how to spot older adults who may be particularly vulnerable to financial abuse and then to refer suspected investment fraud involving these at-risk patients to state securities regulators and/or to APS •"Confessions of a Scam Artist" publication—information to raise awareness Department of Banking •"Protect Yourself, Protect Your Money"— publication includes information on common scams and tips on avoiding scams	Adult Protective Services Agencies •State law grants APS access to bank records for elder financial exploitation investigations PA Securities Commission •ABCs for APS Professionals—information for APS workers on how to identify investment fraud Attorney General •Elder Abuse Unit—investigates and prosecutes elder financial exploitation Philadelphia Police Department	

State	Efforts to Prevent Exploitation by Financial Services Providers, Power-of-Attorney Agents, and Paid in-Home Caregivers	Efforts to Educate and Inform Older Adults and the General Public	Efforts to Provide Information to and Enhance Expertise for Professionals Responding to Exploitation	Efforts to Foster Collaboration among Institutions Responding to Exploitation
			•Crimes Against Retired and Elderly Unit—investigates crimes affecting older adults SeniorLAW Center •Provides legal assistance to senior crime victims	

Source: GAO interviews and review of documents from California, Illinois, New York, and Pennsylvania.

Appendix XI: Examples of Non-Governmental Organization Activities to Prevent and Respond to Elder Financial Exploitation

	Efforts to Prevent Exploitation by Financial Services Providers, Power-of-Attorney Agents, and Paid in-Home Caregivers	Efforts to Educate and Inform Older Adults and the General Public	Efforts to Provide Information to and Enhance Expertise for Professionals Responding to Exploitation	Efforts to Foster Collaboration among Institutions Responding to Exploitation
AARP *AARP is a nonprofit, nonpartisan organization, with a membership of more than 37 million, that helps people age 50 and above have*	Free Lunch Monitor Program •AARP asks members to send them invitations they receive to free lunch seminars that sell investment products.	Protecting Your Assets Project •Project provides basic tips on avoiding fraud to AARP members,	MoSafe Program •In conjunction with the Missouri Bankers Association, the AARP	

(Continued)

	Efforts to Prevent Exploitation by Financial Services Providers, Power-of-Attorney Agents, and Paid in-Home Caregivers	Efforts to Educate and Inform Older Adults and the General Public	Efforts to Provide Information to and Enhance Expertise for Professionals Responding to Exploitation	Efforts to Foster Collaboration among Institutions Responding to Exploitation
independence, choice, and control in ways that are beneficial to them and society as a whole.	Members also attend and report back to AARP on the specific investment offers. AARP has compiled information on the trustworthiness of these investment sales pitches.	including email blasts and website links for additional information No Free Lunch Program •Provides information on responding to high pressure sales tactics on AARP's website, as well as information on senior financial advisor designations Research Projects Related to Elder Financial Exploitation •AARP has conducted several research projects related to elder financial exploitation including studies of:	Missouri state office developed a training program for bank clerks on financial exploitation	

	Efforts to Prevent Exploitation by Financial Services Providers, Power-of-Attorney Agents, and Paid in-Home Caregivers	Efforts to Educate and Inform Older Adults and the General Public	Efforts to Provide Information to and Enhance Expertise for Professionals Responding to Exploitation	Efforts to Foster Collaboration among Institutions Responding to Exploitation
		•personality traits of fraud victims and effective prevention messages, •effective outreach activities for investor fraud victims, •diminished financial capacity of older adults and implications for the financial services industry, •preventing the use of misleading senior designations, •power-of-attorney abuse and what states can do about it, and •background checks and other screenings for home care providers		
American Bar Association *A voluntary professional organization.*		Research Projects Related to Elder Financial Exploitation	Continuing Legal Education Seminars •Webinars on topics related to elder abuse	

(Continued)

	Efforts to Prevent Exploitation by Financial Services Providers, Power-of-Attorney Agents, and Paid in-Home Caregivers	Efforts to Educate and Inform Older Adults and the General Public	Efforts to Provide Information to and Enhance Expertise for Professionals Responding to Exploitation	Efforts to Foster Collaboration among Institutions Responding to Exploitation
The mission of the American Bar Association Commission on Law and Aging is to strengthen and secure the legal rights, dignity, autonomy, quality of life, and quality of care of elders.		•Several research projects related to elder financial exploitation have been conducted, including studies of: •state APS laws and types of elder abuse, •bank employees and their ability to report elder financial exploitation, •court-focused elder abuse initiatives, and •elder abuse registries		
American Bankers Association *Represents banks of all sizes and types and is the voice for the nation's banking industry and its employees*		Protecting the Elderly From Financial Abuse Pamphlet •Pamphlet is designed for older adults and the general public. It includes information on signs of financial abuse, protecting from financial abuse, and what to do if someone suspects financial abuse.	Information formembers •Shares information with members on how to identify elder financial exploitation •Provides information via conferences and phone briefings to its members on federal bank privacy laws, encouraging members to report suspicious activity	

	Efforts to Prevent Exploitation by Financial Services Providers, Power-of-Attorney Agents, and Paid in-Home Caregivers	Efforts to Educate and Inform Older Adults and the General Public	Efforts to Provide Information to and Enhance Expertise for Professionals Responding to Exploitation	Efforts to Foster Collaboration among Institutions Responding to Exploitation
			Frontline Training for Bank Employees •Consumer protection and privacy training is intended for frontline bank employees. Training includes various aspects of consumer protection, including elder financial exploitation. Bank Compliance Magazine article July-August 2011 edition •In a magazine distributed to banks, types of elder financial exploitation, why older adults are particularly vulnerable, the role of banks, and relevant state and federal laws were described	

(Continued)

	Efforts to Prevent Exploitation by Financial Services Providers, Power-of-Attorney Agents, and Paid in-Home Caregivers	Efforts to Educate and Inform Older Adults and the General Public	Efforts to Provide Information to and Enhance Expertise for Professionals Responding to Exploitation	Efforts to Foster Collaboration among Institutions Responding to Exploitation
National Adult Protective Services Association *A national non-profit with over 500 members in all fifty states. Provides state and local Adult Protective Services program administrators and staff with a forum for sharing information, solving problems, and improving the quality of services for victims of elder and vulnerable adult abuse.*		Research Projects Related to Elder Financial Exploitation •Currently conducting a baseline survey of state APS programs •Report on state APS responses to financial exploitation of vulnerable adults	National Adult Protective Services Resource Center •Runs the Resource Center, which is funded by the Administration on Aging National Conference •Hosts a conference for APS professionals and several sessions are usually dedicated to elder financial exploitation Webinars •Hosts webinars on various topics related to elder abuse for APS professionals	

	Efforts to Prevent Exploitation by Financial Services Providers, Power-of-Attorney Agents, and Paid in-Home Caregivers	Efforts to Educate and Inform Older Adults and the General Public	Efforts to Provide Information to and Enhance Expertise for Professionals Responding to Exploitation	Efforts to Foster Collaboration among Institutions Responding to Exploitation
Financial Industry Regulatory Authority *The largest independent regulator for all securities firms doing business in the United States. Its mission is to protect America's investors by making sure the securities industry operates fairly and honestly.*	Collects investor complaints • Investors are able to make complaints via its website, phone, fax, or mail.		Creating APS Core Training •Working with California officials to create core competencies for APS workers, which would include financial exploitation, with a goal of creating national core training for APS workers	Collaboration with federal and state regulators • Works closely with the Securities and Exchange Commission on investor education and examinations • Works with state securities regulators on investor education campaigns Collaboration with other non-governmental organization Together with the Stanford Center on Longevity, founded a financial fraud research center

(Continued)

	Efforts to Prevent Exploitation by Financial Services Providers, Power-of-Attorney Agents, and Paid in-Home Caregivers	Efforts to Educate and Inform Older Adults and the General Public	Efforts to Provide Information to and Enhance Expertise for Professionals Responding to Exploitation	Efforts to Foster Collaboration among Institutions Responding to Exploitation
		Investor Alerts • Disseminates information about scams, trends, or new financial products Research Projects Related to Elder Financial Exploitation Conducted several research projects related to elder financial exploitation, including studies of: • Investment fraud • National Financial Capability Study • Senior Investor Literacy and Fraud Susceptibility • Senior Fraud Risk • Senior Financial Advisor Designations		

	Efforts to Prevent Exploitation by Financial Services Providers, Power-of-Attorney Agents, and Paid in-Home Caregivers	Efforts to Educate and Inform Older Adults and the General Public	Efforts to Provide Information to and Enhance Expertise for Professionals Responding to Exploitation	Efforts to Foster Collaboration among Institutions Responding to Exploitation
Investor Protection Trust *A nonprofit organization devoted to investor education. The primary mission is to provide independent, objective information needed by consumers to make informed investment decisions.*	Elder Investment Fraud and Financial Exploitation Prevention Program • The program educates medical professionals on how to spot older Americans who may be particularly vulnerable to financial abuse, particularly those with mild cognitive impairment, and then to refer suspected investment fraud involving these at-risk patients to state securities regulators and/or to local APS professionals.	Research Projects Related to Elder Financial Exploitation • Surveyed older adults and their families about handling personal finances, current financial conditions, and experiences with financial fraud or abuse. • Surveyed experts about elder financial exploitation. National Call-in Day: Protecting Elders from Financial Abuse • Hosted a call-in day, in collaboration with other organizations, for older adults and their families to receive free advice and guidance on protecting against investment swindles and financial abuse		

(Continued)

	Efforts to Prevent Exploitation by Financial Services Providers, Power-of-Attorney Agents, and Paid in-Home Caregivers	Efforts to Educate and Inform Older Adults and the General Public	Efforts to Provide Information to and Enhance Expertise for Professionals Responding to Exploitation	Efforts to Foster Collaboration among Institutions Responding to Exploitation
Financial Services Roundtable, BITS *The mission of the Financial Services Roundtable is to protect and promote the economic vitality and integrity of its members and the United States financial system. BITS addresses issues at the intersection of financial services, technology and public policy, such as critical infrastructure protection, fraud prevention, and the safety of financial services.*		Older Americans Financial Abuse Prevention Working Group Pamphlet •Contains fraud prevention tips for consumers and for organizations working with older adults	BITS Fraud Prevention Toolkit •Information for banks on the role of financial institutions in preventing and responding to elder financial exploitation, red flags and types of offenders and scams, and the role of APS	Collaboration with stateand local governments and other non-governmental organizations Older Americans Financial Abuse Prevention Working Group

Source: GAO interviews and information collected on organization websites.

APPENDIX XII: CRIMINAL BACKGROUND CHECK REQUIREMENTS FOR IN-HOME CAREGIVERS IN SELECTED STATES

State	Criminal Background Checks Mandatory or Discretionary?	Checks for Publicly Funded Care Only or Publicly and Privately Funded Care?	Type of Background Check	Conditional Employment Allowed?a	Disqualifying Offenses
California	Discretionary	Publicly & privately funded care	State and federal	State does not specify	Offenses that are against dependent or vulnerable individuals or fraud-related
Illinois	Mandatory	Publicly & privately funded care	State only	Yes	Homicide; other violent, sex-related, drug-related, fraud-related; and property offenses
New York	Mandatory	Publicly & privately funded care	State and sometimes federal	Yes	Homicide; other violent, sex-related, drug-related, and fraud-related offenses;and offenses against dependent or vulnerable individuals
Pennsylvania	Mandatory	Publicly & privately funded care	State and sometimes federal	Yes	Homicide; other violent, sex-related , drug-related, and fraud-related offenses;and offenses against dependent or vulnerable individuals

Source: AARP Public Policy Institute. (September 2010) Safe at Home? Developing Effective Criminal Background Checks and Other Screening Policies for Home Care Workers

Note: Information is as of December 2008.

a Conditional employment occurs when in-home caregivers are allowed to begin working before background checks are complete.

APPENDIX XIII: RESOURCE CENTERS SUPPORTED BY THE ADMINISTRATION ON AGING

Name	Intended Users	Information and Services
National Center on Elder Abuse	National, state, and local professionals working with victims of elder mistreatment, including APS professionals, state and federal agencies, law enforcement, legal professionals, health care professionals, domestic violence networks, community-based organizations, elder rights advocates Public policymakers Researchers General public	Disseminates news items related to elder abuse Operates a listserv for professionals Provides information about promising practices and interventions Provides a training library Funds research
National Adult Protective Services Resource Center	Adult Protective Services professionals nationwide	Disseminates a monthly newsletter Maintains an APS-specific listserv Publishes brief descriptions of recent applicable research Holds regular webcasts Collects and compiles detailed information about APS throughout the country Provides information to state and local APS programs to facilitate implementation of identified best practices and research findings
National Legal Resource Center	Professionals involved in protecting the rights of older persons, including: Providers of legal assistance, including senior legal helplines State and local APS professionals Elder rights advocates	Disseminates information on a wide range of legal issuesaffecting older adults Training on legal issues Technical assistance on the provision of legal services to older adults Case consultation, including on elder financial exploitation cases

Source: GAO analysis of information provided by NCEA, National Adult Protective Services Resource Center, and National Legal Resource Center.

APPENDIX XIV: EXAMPLE OF A LETTER PROMOTING A FRAUDULENT SWEEPSTAKES SCHEME

OFFICIAL PRIZE PAYMENT

*** Official signed document established by the prize commission ***

**************************MIXED AADC 07099
3019276677 08485.0.14 15067
MR [redacted]
[redacted] PKWY APT [redacted]
CINCINNATI OH [redacted]

DEFINITIVE FINDINGS AND RESULTS

All information in these financial documents is official.

Mr [redacted], payment of the sum of $ 29,400.00 is 100% SURE. Do not waste any time and return your acceptance form as soon as possible.

After receiving your acceptance form confirmed and recognized winner, I could write the following to you:

1. Here are the definitive results:
   MR [redacted], YOU HAVE REALLY WON!
2. This is no joke. It is true:
   YOU HAVE BEEN CONFIRMED AS THE MAIN WINNER OF A CHECK!*
3. As soon as we receive your declaration of prize acceptance,
   WE GUARANTEE THAT A CHECK WILL BE SENT
   in your name and for
   $ 29,400.00 by registered mail with acknowledgment of receipt to your address in CINCINNATI!

I am very happy for you!

[redacted] Pkwy Apt [redacted]
Cincinnati OH [redacted]
UNITED STATES

We are now waiting for your response before acting!

Attribution No.:
659.001.360
Type of prize to pay:
CHECK
Amount of the check:
$ 29,400.00

Conditions of participation:
You must be at least 18 years old to participate. This is a free contest with no obligation to purchase, in which prize distribution is governed by laws of chance and in which there is one winner and losers. Participation in the contest implies that you accept all the conditions of participation. The contest closes on Dec. 31, 2011. The main prize to be won is $ 29,400.00. Every participant has received several documents, including an acceptance form that is the participation form. In order to be eligible to win, participants must return the acceptance form with or without an order for the Magic Method. This is confirmation of participation. If you also place an order, use the enclosed, pre-addressed reply envelope. If you participate without placing an order, please use a plain white envelope and return your acceptance form directly to the address of Angèle and Angelina. Participation at the same time as placing an order is processed more rapidly to ensure that you rapidly receive the Magic Method and the Cosmic Sigil of the Sun. One participant will be randomly selected among all those who responded, who will be the main winner who may receive the check for $ 29,400.00. All other participants may receive consolation prizes that can also be purchase reduction vouchers. The winner of the main prize of $ 29,400.00 will be informed by registered post and will then have 4 weeks to respond. In the absence of a response, the prize will be definitively lost. If the response is received in time, the prize will be sent to the legitimate winner within 48 hours. All decisions are final. This is an international contest.The chance of winning the main prize is 1/20,000.

*according to the conditions of participation

- 1 -

Source: Postal Inspection Service.

Appendix XV: Total Number of FTC Consumer Sentinel Network Complaints by Source, CY2011

Source	Number of Complaints	Percent of Total
Complaints made directly to the FTC, by individuals andothersa	788,576	43%
Better Business Bureaus	416,520	23%
Internet Crime Complaint Centerb	302,381	17%
Western Union Money Transfer	54,657	3%
Canadian Anti-Fraud Centre	39,260	2%
Publisher's Clearinghouse	37,311	2%
Others (such as state and local agencies and U.S. Postal Inspectors)	174,375	10%
TOTAL	1,813,080	100%

Source: FTC.

[a]These complaints may be made by phone, mail, or on the FTC's website.

[b]The Internet Crime Complaint Center, co-sponsored by the FBI and the National White Collar Crime Center, collects internet-related criminal complaints and aims to further research, develop, and refer these complaints to appropriate federal, state, local, and international agencies.

End Notes

[1] See GAO, Elder Justice: Stronger Federal Leadership Could Enhance National Response to Elder Abuse, GAO-11-208 (Washington, D.C.: March 2, 2011).

[2] MetLife Mature Market Institute et. al., The MetLife Study of Elder Financial Abuse: Crimes of Occasion, Desperation, and Predation against America's Elders (2011). The study assumed that the approximately $530 million in loss from all forms of elder financial abuse occurred at the same rate for the other 9 months of the year. It further assumed that this loss would be the same for the 36 percent of articles about elder financial abuse that the study identified but did not cite a specific dollar figure for.

[3] Gunther, Jilenne, The 2010 Utah Cost of Financial Exploitation, Utah Division of Aging and Adult Services (2012).

[4] Other types of elder abuse include physical, psychological, and sexual abuse, as well as neglect and self-neglect.

[5] Hebert et al., "Alzheimer Disease in the US Population," Archives of Neurology, 60 (August 2003): 1119-1122.

[6] Agarwal et al., "The Age of Reason: Financial Decisions over the Life Cycle with Implications for Regulation," Brookings Papers on Economic Activity 2 (Washington, D.C.: 2009): 51-117.

[7] See appendixes I through IX for additional information on each of these agencies. The Department of Housing and Urban Development (HUD) also functions as a federal

consumer protection agency in that they administer the Home Equity Conversion Mortgage Program, the nation's largest reverse mortgage program for older adults.

[8] Pub. L. 89-73, 79 Stat. 218 (codified as amended at 42 U.S.C. §§ 3001-3058ff).

[9] 42 U.S.C. § 3011(e)(2).

[10] Pub. L. No. 111-148, tit. VI, subtit. H, 124 Stat. 119, 782-804 (2010) (codified at 42 U.S.C. §§ 1320b-25, 1395i-3a, and 1397j-1397m-5). The EJA was enacted as part of the Patient Protection and Affordable Care Act, which was signed into law on March 23, 2010.

[11] § 2042(a)(1)(B) and (2), 124 Stat. 794 (codified at 42 U.S.C. § 1397m-1(a)(1)(B) and (2)).

[12] § 2042(a)(1)(C), 124 Stat. 794 (codified at 42 U.S.C. § 1397m-1(a)(1)(C)).

[13] § 2042(a)(1)(D), 124 Stat. 794 (codified at 42 U.S.C. § 1397m-1(a)(1)(D)).

[14] § 2042(a)(1)(E), 124 Stat. 794 (codified at 42 U.S.C. § 1397m-1(a)(1)(E)).

[15] § 2031, 124 Stat. 790-91 (codified at 42 U.S.C. § 1397l).

[16] § 2042(c), 124 Stat. 795 (codified at 42 U.S.C. 1397m-1(c)).

[17] §§ 2021 and 2022, 124 Stat. 786-89 (codified at 42 U.S.C. §§ 1397k and 1397k-1).

[18] The Corporation for National and Community Service is a federal agency that engages Americans in service through Senior Corps, AmeriCorps, and the Social Innovation Fund. 42 U.S.C. § 12651.

[19] Pub. L. No. 111-203, § 1015, 124 Stat. 1376, 1974 (2010) (codified at 12 U.S.C. § 5495).

[20] § 1013(g)(1), 124 Stat. 1973 (codified at 12 U.S.C. § 5493(g)(1)).

[21] See appendix X for examples of activities undertaken by APS, criminal justice, and consumer protection agencies in California, Illinois, New York, and Pennsylvania to prevent elder financial exploitation by financial services providers, power of attorney agents, and in-home caregivers. See appendix XI for examples of these activities undertaken by private organizations.

[22] Financial planners can provide a variety of services, including preparing financial plans for clients based on their financial circumstances and objectives and making recommendations for specific actions clients may take. In many cases, financial planners also help implement these recommendations by, for example, selling investment products, such as insurance, securities, or other investments. Financial planners are subject to federal and state regulation pertaining to investment advisers, broker-dealers, and insurance agents, depending on the services they provide. See GAO, Consumer Finance: Regulatory Coverage Generally Exists for Financial Planners, but Consumer Protection Issues Remain, GAO-11-235 (Washington, D.C.: January 18, 2011).

[23] Broker-dealers handle trades between the buyers and sellers of securities and charge a fee to do so. Broker-dealers may buy securities from customers or sell from their own inventory. Most are also members of the Financial Industry Regulatory Authority (FINRA). FINRA is a self-regulatory organization with oversight of all broker-dealers doing business with the public in the United States.

[24] Insurance agents sell products, such as life insurance or annuities. They must be licensed by the states to sell these products and are subject to state insurance regulation. The sale of variable insurance products, such as variable life insurance or variable annuities, is subject to both state insurance regulation and broker-dealer regulation. See GAO-11-235.

[25] NASAA is a national membership organization for state securities regulators.

[26] See GAO-11-235.

[27] SEC, FINRA, and NASAA, Protecting Senior Investors: Report on Examinations of Securities Firms Providing "Free Lunch" Sales Seminars (2007).

[28] SEC, Guide for Seniors: Protect Yourself Against Investment Fraud; SEC, FINRA, and NASAA, Investor Alert, Investment Products and Sales Practices Commonly Used to Defraud Seniors: Stories from the Frontline.

[29] SEC, Guide for Seniors: Protect Yourself Against Investment Fraud.

[30] CFPB, "Request for Information Regarding Senior Financial Exploitation," 77 Fed. Reg. 36,491 (June 19, 2012).

[31] The Uniform Law Commission is a state-supported organization that drafts model legislation to promote clarity and stability to critical areas of state statutory law.

[32] According to the Uniform Law Commission, Alabama, Arkansas, Colorado, Idaho, Maine, Montana, Nebraska, Nevada, New Mexico, Ohio, Virginia, West Virginia, and Wisconsin have adopted the Uniform Power of Attorney Act.

[33] See GAO, Guardianships: Cases of Financial Exploitation, Abuse, and Neglect of Seniors, GAO-10-1046 (Washington, D.C.: September 30, 2010), and GAO, Incapacitated Adults: Oversight of Federal Fiduciaries and Court-Appointed Guardians Needs Improvement, GAO-11-678 (Washington, D.C.: July 22, 2011).

[34] OAA Title III-B provides funding for in-home services, such as personal care, chore, and homemaker assistance.

[35] 42 U.S.C. § 1396d(a)(7). Medicaid is a joint federal-state financing program for health care services for certain low-income individuals. State Medicaid programs may cover home-based care, such as personal care and homemaker services, for Medicaid beneficiaries who need help with self-care due to disabilities or health conditions.

[36] According to AoA, many of those who exploit older adults are informal or family caregivers who are not employed or subject to background checks and this may be a more difficult type of exploitation to prevent.

[37] States must enact standards for provider participation to ensure that providers are qualified, effective, and cost-efficient, and to protect program beneficiaries. At the same time, these requirements must not unfairly restrict participation in the Medicaid program. As long as states meet these criteria, they have significant latitude in specifying their provider qualification requirements. AARP Public Policy Institute, Safe at Home? Developing Effective Criminal Background Checks and Other Screening Policies for Home Care Workers (September 2010).

[38] National Conference of State Legislatures, State Policies on Criminal Background Checks for Medicaid-Supported In-Home Direct Care Workers (December 18, 2008).

[39] See appendix XII for examples of background check requirements for in-home caregivers in the four states we reviewed.

[40] See AARP Public Policy Institute, Safe at Home?

[41] Pub. L. No. 111-148, tit. VI, subtit. C, § 6201, 124 Stat. 119, 721.

[42] In addition to criminal background checks, APS agencies in several states maintain a registry of elder abuse offenders that can be used to flag in-home caregivers who might financially exploit older adults.

[43] See appendix X for examples of activities undertaken by APS, criminal justice, and consumer protection agencies in California, Illinois, New York, and Pennsylvania to educate and inform older adults about elder financial exploitation. See appendix XI for examples of these activities undertaken by private organizations.

[44] 42 U.S.C. § 3011(e)(2).

[45] See GAO, Results-Oriented Government: Practices that Can Help Enhance and Sustain Collaboration Among Federal Agencies, GAO-06-15, (Washington, D.C.: October 21, 2005).

[46] The Financial Services Roundtable is an advocacy group with members from the banking, securities, investment, and insurance sectors. It aims to protect and promote the economic vitality and integrity of its members and the U.S. financial system.

[47] See appendix X for examples of activities undertaken by APS, criminal justice, and consumer protection agencies in California, Illinois, New York, and Pennsylvania to build additional expertise. See appendix XI for examples of these activities undertaken by private organizations.

[48] Forensic accountants specialize in investigating financial crimes. The Certified Fraud Examiner credential is one professional designation that a forensic accountant may hold.

[49] § 2042(a)(1)(C), 124 Stat. 794, 1397m-1(a)(1)(C).

[50] See appendix XIII for more information on AoA resource centers.

[51] 42 U.S.C. § 3011(e)(2)(a)(ix).

[52] See Adria E. Navarro et al., "Holding Abusers Accountable: An Elder Abuse Forensic Center Increases Criminal Prosecution of Financial Exploitation" (funded by Justice), The Gerontologist, vol. 0, (May 15, 2012). This study was funded by Justice.

[53] See appendix X for examples of activities undertaken by APS, criminal justice, and consumer protection agencies in California, Illinois, New York, and Pennsylvania to support collaboration. See appendix XI for examples of these activities undertaken by private organizations.

[54] Brandl et al., Elder Abuse Detection and Intervention (New York: 2007).

[55] Mass-marketing fraud refers generally to any type of fraud scheme that uses one or more mass communication techniques and technologies—such as the Internet, telephones, the mail, and even mass meetings in person—to contact, solicit, and obtain funds or other items of value from multiple victims in one or more jurisdictions. See appendix XIV for an example of a letter promoting a sweepstakes scam.

[56] The Internet Crime Complaint Center is an online system that collects complaints of suspected criminal or civil Internet-related violations and develops referrals to law enforcement and regulatory agencies at the federal, state, local, tribal, and international levels. It is a partnership between the FBI and the National White Collar Crime Center, a nonprofit that supports the investigation and prosecution of economic and high-tech crime.

[57] According to the Fraud Section of Justice's Criminal Division, lottery scam perpetrators are operating from a growing number of countries, including Costa Rica, the Dominican Republic, Jamaica, the Netherlands, Nigeria, and Spain.

[58] In addition to the work of individual agencies, the Financial Fraud Enforcement Task Force—a broad coalition of more than 20 federal agencies, 94 U.S. Attorneys' Offices, and state and local partners—was created by executive order to (1) investigate and prosecute significant financial crimes and other violations related to the current financial crisis and economic recovery efforts, (2) recover the proceeds of such crimes and violations, and (3) ensure just and effective punishment of those who perpetrate such crimes and violations. Exec. Order No. 13,519, 74 Fed. Reg. 60,123 (Nov. 19, 2009). The Consumer Protection Working Group formed under the Task Force in early 2012 focuses on strengthening the government's collective efforts to address consumer-related scams targeting vulnerable populations.

[59] FTC's Consumer Sentinel Network is an online database that houses millions of consumer complaints available to law enforcement. Sentinel's roster of 28 current data contributors includes 12 state attorneys general, the FBI's Internet Crime Complaint Center, and the Council of Better Business Bureaus. More than 2,600 users from over 2,000 law

enforcement agencies worldwide use the system to share information, prosecute cases, conduct investigations, and pursue leads.

[60] The Illinois Department on Aging designed and administered the training protocol and the Illinois Department of Financial and Professional Regulation certifies compliance with the training requirement.

[61] Most states require some classes of professionals or organizations to report suspected elder abuse, which may include financial exploitation of older individuals, to state authorities. Some states, including California—a state we contacted—specifically include banks as mandatory reporters. Cal. Welf. & Inst. Code § 15630.1 (2012). Some states immunize individuals who make such reports in good faith from civil and/or criminal liability under state law.

[62] § 1031, 124 Stat. 1979-80 (12 U.S.C. § 5531).

[63] Testimony before the Subcommittee on Financial Institutions and Consumer Protection United States Senate Committee on Banking, Housing, and Urban Affairs (Washington, D.C., November 15, 2011).

[64] 31 U.S.C. § 5318(h)(1)(C), 12 C.F.R. § 21.3(a)(3), and pt. 30, app. B (2012).

[65] 31 C.F.R. § 1020.320(a) (2012). If a financial institution knows, suspects, or has reason to suspect, for example, that transactions have no business or apparent lawful purpose or are not the sort in which a particular customer would normally be expected to engage, and the financial institution knows of no reasonable explanation for the transaction after examining the available facts, including the background and possible purpose of the transaction, the financial institution must file a SAR.

[66] FinCEN stores SARs in a database and each state has a law enforcement point-ofcontact with access to the database. Local police and district attorneys rely on their state's FinCEN point-of-contact to obtain SAR information. While SARs could contain leads on elder financial exploitation cases, local officials we spoke with said they did not use SARs often to build criminal cases and SARs are not a vehicle for fast action.

[67] Local criminal justice agencies said that they are able to obtain bank records with a subpoena or search warrant, but banks sometimes take a long time to provide the records. This, in turn, extends already time-intensive investigations.

[68] The American Bar Association completed a report on this issue and concluded that federal privacy laws do not prohibit banks from sharing information in suspected cases of elder financial exploitation. American Bar Association, Can Bank Tellers Tell? Legal Issues Relating to Banks Reporting Financial Abuse of the Elderly (2003).

[69] Pub. L. No. 95-630, tit. XI, 92 Stat. 3641, 3697-3710 (codified as amended at 12 U.S.C. §§ 3401-3422).

[70] Pub. L. No. 106-102, §§ 501-510, 113 Stat. 1338, 1436-1445 (codified as amended at 15 U.S.C. §§ 6801-6809).

[71] See Gunther, "The 2010 Utah Cost of Financial Exploitation."

[72] 42 U.S.C. § 3012(e)(2)(A)(iii) and (iv), and (16).

[73] § 2042(a)(1)(B), 124 Stat. 794 (codified at 42 U.S.C. 1397m-1(a)(1)(B)).

[74] See GAO-11-208.

[75] FTC (2012) Consumer Sentinel Network Data Book for January - December 2011.

[76] See appendix XV for additional information on the data in the Consumer Sentinel Network.

[77] See GAO-11-208.

End Notes for Appendix I

[1] On April 16, 2012, AoA became part of the Administration for Community Living, which also includes HHS's Office on Disability and Administration on Developmental Disabilities.

In: Financial Exploitation of Elders
Editor: Maxime Faubert
ISBN: 978-1-62417-904-4

Chapter 2

STATEMENT OF SENATOR HERBERT KOHL. HEARING ON "AMERICA'S INVISIBLE EPIDEMIC: PREVENTING ELDER FINANCIAL ABUSE"*

Good Afternoon. I would like to thank our witnesses and welcome everyone.

Today we will be talking about ways to prevent a growing national crisis – elder financial abuse. From the opportunistic thief working as a home care aide, to the shady telemarketer who befriends a lonely senior on the phone to take advantage of him through a sweepstakes scam – the stories this Committee has heard are alarming.

Seniors are being victimized every day and the problem is getting worse. According to the Investor Protection Trust, one out of every five older Americans has already been duped by a financial scam. And while the costs associated with elder financial abuse are estimated to be $2.9 billion each year, financial abuse often goes unrecognized because victims are too afraid or embarrassed to report the crime to the authorities.

The reality is, many of us may know an older adult who is at risk, or who has been, a victim of elder financial abuse—it might be a family member, a neighbor, or a friend. In fact, someday it might be you.

---

* This is an edited, reformatted and augmented version of testimony given on November 15, 2012 before the Senate Special Committee on Aging.

But there is hope. Today we will highlight new elder financial abuse prevention programs being implemented across the federal, state, and private sectors. In addition, we will address ways that older Americans can take steps to protect themselves and their assets.

We will start today's hearing with Mr. Frank Abagnale who earned a "Hollywood-worthy" reputation for conning unsuspecting victims. He has come here to share tips for preventing identity theft and protecting against financial fraud.

We will also hear testimony from the Consumer Financial Protection Bureau, a member of the new Elder Justice Coordinating Council. Finally, our panelists from the Financial Services Roundtable and the San Diego County District Attorney's Office will share their knowledge of prevention activities taking place in private banking institutions and at the state-level.

Over the years, I've seen our nation take great strides to combat elder financial abuse – from the passage of the Elder Justice Act, to the creation of a background check system for nursing home employees. It's time to build on our efforts to remedy this invisible epidemic and break the cycle of stigma attached to this horrible crime.

Thank you again to everyone for being here.

In: Financial Exploitation of Elders
Editor: Maxime Faubert ISBN: 978-1-62417-904-4

Chapter 3

TESTIMONY OF FRANK W. ABAGNALE, AUTHOR AND CONSULTANT, ABAGNALE AND ASSOCIATES. HEARING ON "AMERICA'S INVISIBLE EPIDEMIC: PREVENTING ELDER FINANCIAL ABUSE"*

INTODUCTION

Chairman Kohl, Ranking Member Corker, Members of the Committee, I am honored to be invited to testify before you today on the seriousness of identity theft and financial fraud against the elderly and the need for education. I am Frank Abagnale subject of the book, movie and Broadway musical "Catch Me If You Can".

I have a unique perspective having committed fraud as a teenager some 40 years ago and having spent the last 36 years of my life teaching at the FBI Academy and field offices of the Federal Bureau of Investigation. In my 36 year career, I have conducted over 3,000 lectures and written four books on these subjects. For the past 36 years, I have worked to try to prevent fraud, forgery, embezzlement, identity theft and other white collar crimes.

One serious issue we face is financial fraud against the elderly. This can be perpetrated by family members, financial advisers, home healthcare

* This is an edited, reformatted and augmented version of testimony given on November 15, 2012 before the Senate Special Committee on Aging.

providers, friends, scam artists, and others. As I'm sure you are all aware, in 2010 the Consumer Financial Protection Board estimated $2.9 billion dollars was stolen from financially exploited elders and the instances of financial theft from seniors grew 12% from 2008 - 2010. This is probably a low estimate because many times the elderly are too embarrassed to admit that they have been defrauded and therefore it goes unreported. Their families may not even be told. Last year, white collar crime in America had reached the $900 billion dollar mark. Medicare fraud alone was estimated conservatively at $179 billion dollars. The IRS paid over $5 billion dollars in fraudulent tax refunds filed by individuals using a stolen social security number.

I make my home in Charleston, SC. Last month 3.5 million social security numbers and over 300,000 credit and debit card numbers were stolen from the SC Department of Tax Revenue by criminals who hacked into the state's computer system. It is believed that they not only stole social security numbers and credit card information, but also the entire return of each person who filed a SC tax return. This means the criminals have the social security number of the dependents; the home address; bank account numbers and copies of the W-2s. What is truly amazing to an individual like me is that what I did 40 years ago as a teenager is 4,000 times easier to do today due to technology. Unfortunately technology breeds crime -- always has and always will.

There will always be individuals who will use technology in a negative and self-serving way.

I have always believed that the government should take the lead in education to combat this horrendous crime. However, sometimes it seems the government makes it easier for individuals to commit these crimes. For example. The Centers for Medicare and Medicaid Services uses Social Security Numbers as part of the Medicare number. This means that anyone who sees the Medicare number can determine the Social Security Number. In a hospital or medical setting, a worker could have complete access to a senior's Social Security Number, home address, date of birth, possibly credit card numbers, bank account, and other information. This threat of identity theft of seniors will not be alleviated until the Social Security Number is removed from the Medicare card.

The elderly are hungry for information but do not know about legitimate resources where they can turn for help. Numerous companies on television and radio, as well as talk show hosts, promote and market solutions which may or may not actually work. This is a great example of the victim going for help, but being victimized again by those companies that are claiming to help them.

Throughout my career, I have always believed that education is the best prevention. If you educate and explain to people their risks, in most cases they are smart enough to take that information and reduce their risks. I believe education is the only approach to help eliminate elder fraud. Education is not only important for our seniors, but it also helps bring awareness to all citizens so they can recognize the signs of fraud and know how to protect themselves. I believe that one of the most powerful tools at the government's disposal is creative Public Service Announcements that point out the most common scams and explain how to avoid becoming a victim.

I recommend the government sponsor Public Service Announcements, mailing stuffers and educational materials so that individuals can learn to protect themselves and their loved ones.

Protecting one's identity is an individual's responsibility. If a person ages to the point that they cannot take care of their personal issues then the family and friends should help take responsibility. Everyone has to be educated. Government regulation is not the answer.

I recommend the following to seniors to protect their identity:

- Review your credit report semi-annually
- Reconcile your bank accounts in a timely manner
- Be suspicious of calls, e-mails or letters asking for personal information
- Don't give out your SSN - Just because a form contains a space for your SSN doesn't mean you have to provide it.
- Invest in a micro-cut shredder.

Finally, I believe that punishment for fraud and identity theft and recovery of stolen funds are so rare, prevention is the only viable course of action.

In: Financial Exploitation of Elders
Editor: Maxime Faubert
ISBN: 978-1-62417-904-4

Chapter 4

TESTIMONY OF HUBERT H. "SKIP" HUMPHREY III, ASSISTANT DIRECTOR, OFFICE FOR OLDER AMERICANS, CONSUMER FINANCIAL PROTECTION BUREAU. HEARING ON "AMERICA'S INVISIBLE EPIDEMIC: PREVENTING ELDER FINANCIAL ABUSE"*

Thank you Chairman Kohl, Ranking Member Corker, and distinguished members of the Committee for the opportunity to speak with you today about the Office for Older Americans at the Consumer Financial Protection Bureau (Bureau or CFPB) and its work to address the devastating problem of elder financial exploitation.

Chairman Kohl, on the eve of your retirement from the Senate, we want to thank you for your longstanding dedication and the important role you've played as Chairman of this Committee in enhancing the well-being of our older citizens.

My name is Hubert Humphrey and I joined the Bureau in October, 2011, to serve as Assistant Director in the Office for Older Americans. In fact, exactly one year ago today, I had my first opportunity to testify before a Senate committee about the Bureau's important role in helping older

* This is an edited, reformatted and augmented version of testimony given on November 15, 2012 before the Senate Special Committee on Aging.

Americans. Before arriving at the Bureau, as Attorney General in Minnesota—and then as a national board member of AARP—I became keenly aware of the many financial challenges that older consumers face.

CFPB Office for Older Americans

During the past year, I've been privileged to lead an Office with a critically important mission: the CFPB's Office for Older Americans is the only federal office specifically dedicated to the financial health of Americans aged 62 and older.

Our Office works closely with all Divisions of the Bureau to carry out its broad mission: to ensure that markets for consumer financial products and services are fair, transparent, and competitive, and that all consumers have access to those markets.

The Bureau will fulfill this statutory charge by making rules more effective, by consistently and fairly enforcing those rules, and by empowering consumers to take more control over their economic lives.

Our Office's statutory mandate is to help provide consumers aged 62 and over with the tools they need to protect themselves from financial abuse and to make sound financial decisions.

To carry out Congress' directives, in our first year we have made preventing, detecting and redressing elder financial exploitation Job Number One.

To do so, we recognize that collaboration is critical -- on the local, state, and national levels, and between both public and private sectors. We agree with GAO that a collaborative and coordinated effort by federal agencies can help optimize strategies to combat the devastation of elder financial exploitation. Congress already recognized the importance of collaboration when it mandated that the Office for Older Americans do two key things:

- Coordinate consumer protection efforts of seniors with other Federal agencies and State regulators, as appropriate, to promote consistent, effective and efficient enforcement; and
- Work with community organizations, non-profit organizations, and other entities that are involved with educating or assisting seniors.

To jumpstart and foster these collaborative efforts, I have spent the past year traveling throughout the country to meet with state and Tribal officials, such as Attorneys General, financial regulators, Adult Protective Services administrators, commissioners on aging, chief justices, and court administrators, to listen to their experiences and insights, to brainstorm with them about how best to prevent elder financial abuse, to develop joint efforts, and to assure them of my commitment to work with them to protect older Americans from devastating financial losses. I, or a member of my small team, have visited 24 states in just over a year.

Similarly, my staff and I have engaged with non-profits, community organizations and industry groups to figure out how our new federal agency can best help and partner with them, and to begin to share resources to support their work.

For example, we participate in a working group with the Financial Services Roundtable that addresses issues such as enhancing the capacity of financial institutions to report suspected elder financial abuse. We worked closely with the National Endowment for Financial Education on convening a forum of national experts on diminished capacity to make financial decisions.

ELDER JUSTICE COORDINATING COUNCIL

Our Office has been engaged from the outset in coordinating and building cooperative plans with our Federal partners. We applaud the Secretary of Health and Human Services for convening the Elder Justice Coordinating Council in partnership with the Attorney General.

As a member of this eleven-agency body, the Bureau is fully engaged in the Council's work and hopes the Council will shine a light on the disastrous impact of financial exploitation and catalyze the development of a prevention strategy. We recognize the key role in the Council played by HHS Assistant Secretary for Aging Kathy Greenlee, who has been an important partner since I arrived at the Bureau.

At the Elder Justice Coordinating Council's inaugural meeting in October of this year, we heard some important themes from national experts from law enforcement, social services, academia, medicine, law, the judiciary, financial institutions and other stakeholders. These themes include the following:

- Older Americans are victimized by a broad range of perpetrators, including scam artists, family members, caregivers, financial advisers, home repair contractors, and fiduciaries such as agents under power of attorney and court-appointed guardians. Development of strategies to deal with the myriad of "bad actors" is essential.

- There is a need for collaboration at the federal, state and local level, as well as public-private partnerships.
- Diminished capacity to make financial and personal decisions is, as a leading geriatrician and researcher stated, the "800-pound gorilla" in the room.[1] Even mild cognitive impairment disastrously reduces an older adult's ability to detect a fraud or scam. Unfortunately, diminished capacity also undermines the effectiveness of educating older consumers on how to protect themselves.
- It is vital to collect more and better quality data on elder abuse, and to conduct research and evaluate promising tools for prevention, detection and redress.
- We need a broad-scale public education campaign to raise awareness of elder financial abuse and what to do about it. Advocates often make the point that efforts to address elder abuse are thirty years behind the child abuse field—yet we're approaching 50 million seniors aged 62 and over, comprising roughly 20 percent of our population, and all are potential victims.

Office for Older Americans' Initiatives

The CFPB's Office for Older Americans has a number of initiatives underway aimed at combatting elder financial exploitation.

Many already address issues flagged for us and our federal partners at the Elder Justice Coordinating Council. Here are a few:

- We are developing a set of **guides for "lay fiduciaries."** We recognize that family members and other fiduciaries often have no experience handling someone else's money, and they need help so they can do the right thing. These user-friendly "how-to" guides will be for agents under powers of attorney, guardians, trustees, Social Security representative payees, and VA fiduciaries. The Bureau will produce a generic national guide in addition to some state-specific guides and a replication manual for other states. They will explain what a fiduciary does, as well as record-keeping, prudent investment requirements, limitations on comingling funds, and other critical basics to manage a vulnerable adult's money. In addition to this essential guidance on how to handle another person's finances, the guides will teach people to spot financial exploitation and protect assets from unfair, deceptive, and abusive practices by third parties. We anticipate publishing these guides in 2013.

- Another project focuses on **financial exploitation of elders in congregate settings.** Often when older adults residing in these settings are the victims of financial abuse of all types, the first sign may be that their bills for their residences aren't getting paid and they are threatened with eviction. These settings include senior housing, assisted living, and skilled nursing facilities. We are producing a national guide to provide operators of congregate facilities with skills to identify and intervene in exploitation cases further upstream and to have protocols for doing so. We already have offers from many national organizations and government entities to help distribute these much-anticipated guides, and similar enthusiastic responses regarding the lay fiduciary guides.
- The Office is developing a new program called **Money Smart for Older Adults,** in collaboration with the FDIC. This community education and awareness program will focus on preventing, recognizing and reporting elder financial exploitation and will serve as training for older consumers, family caregivers and other key audiences. Partnering with another federal entity will extend the reach of this endeavor.
- On the state and local level, we are working with key stakeholders in several states to help create and sustain **"Older American Protection Networks."** These coalitions aim to develop multi-disciplinary teams to provide community education, raise public awareness, enhance response to reports of abuse, and increase prosecution.
- The Bureau has heard concerns and questions from financial institutions as to whether sharing personal account holder information when reporting elder financial exploitation is permissible under federal law. The Office for Older Americans, in collaboration with other Bureau offices, is developing strategies for communicating clearly to a spectrum of financial institutions that the Gramm-Leach-Bliley Act generally does not prohibit them from reporting suspected abuse to—or respond to requests for personal information from—law enforcement, APS agencies, and other relevant entities. In addition, the Bureau is exploring options for collaborating with other federal agencies in providing this guidance to financial institutions. Through

its efforts, the Bureau hopes to convey that these actions are permissible and important.

OTHER FEDERAL EFFORTS

Through our outreach efforts and our initial work in the Elder Justice Coordinating Council, we've learned that our federal partners have many initiatives that complement ours and that, taken together, can make a real difference in public education and prevention of financial exploitation. These partners include the Administration on Aging at HHS, the Social Security Administration, the U.S. Postal Inspection Service, the Department of Housing and Urban Development, the Department of the Treasury, the Department of Justice, the Federal Trade Commission, the Department of Veterans Affairs, the Department of Labor, the Corporation for National and Community Service, and the Securities and Exchange Commission.

CONCLUSION

Congressional leadership and support is critical to implementing a multi-faceted solution to the serious problem of elder financial exploitation. We commend the Chairman, the ranking member and other members of this Committee for holding this hearing to put the issue in the spotlight. We know that this is just one in a series of hearings you have convened to examine various aspects of the problem. We look forward to continued information sharing with members of Congress and the GAO on this important topic.

Again, thank you for the opportunity to present this testimony.

End Note

[1] Oral statement of Dr. Mark Lachs, Weill Medical College of Cornell University and Director, New York City Elder Abuse Center, October 11, 2012.

In: Financial Exploitation of Elders
Editor: Maxime Faubert
ISBN: 978-1-62417-904-4

Chapter 5

STATEMENT OF PAUL SMOCER, PRESIDENT, BITS, FINANCIAL SERVICES ROUNDTABLE. HEARING ON "AMERICA'S INVISIBLE EPIDEMIC: PREVENTING ELDER FINANCIAL ABUSE"*

INTRODUCTION

The Financial Services Roundtable[1] (the "Roundtable") and BITS appreciate the opportunity to share our thoughts with the members of the Senate Special Committee on Aging regarding the financial exploitation of older Americans and actions we can collectively take to reduce that exploitation.

The financial services industry is a key part of the circle protecting older Americans from financial fraud and exploitation. When employees observe signs of potential exploitation, they can work with families, caregivers, social service agencies and law enforcement to prevent, detect, and help investigate and prosecute the individuals who engage in fraud.

The Roundtable and its members are committed to encouraging their employees comply with high standards of conduct when providing financial advice to all customers, including older Americans and their families.

* This is an edited, reformatted and augmented version of testimony given on November 15, 2012 before the Senate Special Committee on Aging.

Helping ensure a secure retirement for millions of Americans is central to the business and the mission of the financial services industry.

THE PROBLEM

By 2030, the number of Americans aged 65 and older is projected to double to 71 million, roughly 20 percent of the U.S. population.[2] In some states, fully a quarter of the population is likely to be aged 65 and older.[3] Unfortunately, this increase in the aging population creates a potentially large pool of potential victims for financial exploitation.

It is sad, but true, that the most frequent perpetrators of financial abuse are family members, who by some estimates commit nearly 75% of crimes,[4] and professional criminals. It is also important to note that financial institutions are often the first line of defense against this financial exploitation.

Since many older customers prefer to conduct transactions in person, financial services employees can be the first to detect changes in an older customer's behavior.

Signs of exploitation of an elderly customer may include unusual transactions or changes to accounts, unpaid bills, changes in spending patterns, new individuals accompanying the customer to a bank facility, and missing property. When these and other signs are detected, and an investigation suggests that exploitation is taking place, financial institutions can help the customer take action to protect his or her assets. Financial institutions also work with agencies such as Adult Protective Services (APS), local law enforcement and prosecutors, many times as part of local or regional task forces focused on elder abuse prevention and prosecution.

Institutions also report suspected abuse via the Suspicious Activity Reports (SARs) filed with the Financial Crimes Enforcement Network (FinCEN), an agency of the United States Department of the Treasury.

Following the filing of SARs, institutions may be contacted by law enforcement who are investigating the case. Institutions actively work with law enforcement after filing all legally required documents. Institutions also participate in regional partnerships that involve law enforcement of all levels. During these meetings, institutions will share trends and suspects.

This allows for institutions and law enforcement partners to share best practices. Through this active engagement and partnership, cases are able to be more quickly resolved.

For decades, financial institutions have been at the forefront of fraud detection utilizing sophisticated technology, modeling, training and education. Because of these proactive measures, they are often the first to detect patterns associated with fraud.

Using a variety of safeguards, financial institutions make every attempt to ensure the reliability and security of financial transactions as well as protect financial privacy. In fact, financial institutions often exceed the standards set by financial regulators in order to protect their customers, shareholders and employees better.

Education – of employees, customers and other stakeholders – is critical for preventing financial abuse of all customers – including more vulnerable ones such as older Americans. Many financial institutions have extensive programs to educate employees and customers on detecting abuse and steps to secure accounts from the lure of fraudsters.

Financial institutions also work closely with APS, law enforcement and prosecutors to educate those entities on patterns of fraudulent activity and help identify individual cases of potential fraud. Financial institutions also work closely with community organizations to host panel discussions and community events to educate seniors and their caregivers about the risk of elder financial abuse.

These efforts provide older American and their advocates education and resources to not only recognize financial elder abuse, but to also take steps to proactively protect oneself and ones assets through, for example, proper document disposal and identity theft prevention, and reports of the crime when it occurs.

Employees and customers who are better educated about fraudulent behavior and preventing fraud are more likely to take fraud prevention measures. An example of the Roundtable member's education efforts is a white paper produced by the Roundtable's BITS group entitled, "*Protecting the Elderly and Vulnerable from Financial Fraud and Exploitation,*" which helps financial institutions and their customers identify and combat elder abuse.[5]

The Roundtable also partnered with the Administration for Community Living/Department of Health and Human Services and the Consumer Financial Protection Bureau to support the June 14, 2012 White House Office of Public Engagement symposium in recognition of the 7th annual World Elder Abuse Awareness Day by providing financial industry speakers for the panel addressing the prevention of elder financial abuse.

Recognizing the scope of this issue, the Roundtable's member believe it is important to continue to focus on it and to bring resources to bear. To that end, the Roundtable's members have formed a working group to focus on the issue of preventing financial abuse of the elderly. Further recognizing that solutions will require a multi-faceted approach, the Group's members consist not only of financial institutions, but additionally of a collaborative cross-section of federal agency representatives, representatives from various adult protective services organizations, and academics focused on the area of elder abuse.

The Elder Working Group currently has identified two key projects on which it will concentrate. These are:

- Develop a structure/syllabus for training financial institution consumer-facing staff and all new hires on elder fraud trends and internal procedures for reacting to suspected elder financial abuse, including engaging Adult Protective Services and law enforcement. This work will focus on building on work done previously, will incorporate new learnings and research and broaden the educational base for employees. Once completed, the work will be shared openly across the financial services sector.
- Work with financial institutions with strong education programs to develop a publicly available awareness and education program to be made available to all financial institutions.

Challenges and Impediments

As we have engaged in our efforts regarding prevention of elder financial abuse and based on the experiences and feedback of financial institutions, we have identified a number of areas where potential impediments exist to improving prevention.

For many of those, the assistance of the agencies forming the Elder Justice Coordinating Council (EJCC), either directly or in concert with other non-EJCC agencies, would be helpful to clarify concerns or remove impediments. On October 11, 2012, I had the opportunity to present these ideas to the agencies involved in the EJCC at its inaugural meeting. The impediments and possible solutions include:

- Clarify the permissibility of age-based fraud monitoring. As noted previously, financial institutions utilize sophisticated fraud detection technology and modeling in their attempts to prevent and identify potential fraudulent activity in an attempt to protect customers. An added layer of sophistication could be to segregate their elder customers' activities for special screening. Many financial institutions are concerned, however, that segregating their customer population for this purpose could be interpreted to place them in violation of existing age discrimination laws and, therefore, put the institution at risk for potential fines or regulatory actions.

It would be extremely beneficial if the involved EJCC agencies, particularly the Department of Justice, could clarify permissibility of age-based fraud monitoring. If such segregation is currently permissible, to assuage the concerns we have heard, a written opinion of the permissibility would be extremely helpful. If, in fact, it is considered a violation of current anti-discrimination laws to segregate this population for fraud monitoring purposes, we encourage the EJCC to undertake an effort to pursue legislative action to allow for an exception.

- Authority to authorize a protective hold on a suspicious transaction. One significant challenge financial institution employees encounter is situations where an elderly customer wants to perform a transaction (e.g., a withdrawal, a request to transfer funds) in a situation where the employee strongly suspects or even knows that fraud is involved. This clearly creates a conundrum pitting the financial institution's contractual obligation to carry out its customers and instructions and the financial institutions' desire to prevent the elderly customer from being defrauded.

There are a few methods that are suggested for dealing with this issue:

- Working with CFPB and Treasury create an option allowing institutions to put a minimal hold on the transaction pending the sending of an alert of APS and APS discussing the situation with the customer. It will likely be necessary for CFPB and Treasury to work with the states to implement this suggestion.
- Working collaboratively with input from the U.S. Department of Justice, U.S. Postal Inspection Service, Federal Trade Commission and other agencies along with input from financial institutions, create and maintain a list of known fraudulent actors

that can be used to "convince" elders of their involvement in a fraudulent situation.

- Leverage the work already underway and led by the Consumer Financial Protection Bureau to create a list of local and regional APS services into a shareable database that financial institutions could use to understand who to contact that might be helpful in discussing these types of situations with involved elders. Along with creating a database for contacts, it will be necessary to further clarify the type of information institutions are legally able to share with APS regarding their older customer.

- Another substantial challenge occurs when an individual with a duly executed Power of Attorney to act on behalf of an elder is suspected of trying to perpetrate fraudulent activity or activity not in the best interest of the elder. Duly executed Powers of Attorney give the holder the legal right to act on behalf of the customer. This essentially creates the same conundrum for the financial institution as noted in the previous point.

There are a series of actions we would ask the EJCC members to consider regarding this issue. They include:

- Powers of Attorney laws and regulations vary by state and, particularly in the case of Durable Powers of Attorney, can involve granting rights to the agent even after the principal becomes incapacitated. While the agent is obligated to exercise due care and protect the principal, state law is not uniform with respect to the specific responsibilities of an agent with regard to financial transactions, particularly when the principal is an elder. The development of uniform state laws and a Uniform Power of Attorney would be very helpful. Study of the feasibility and benefits of having a uniform Power of Attorney, particularly one for situations in which the principle is an elder should be undertaken.
- Select agencies – most likely U.S. Department of Health and Human Services, Social Security Administration, CFPB, U.S. Department of Justice, the Federal Trade Commission and the U.S. Department of Veterans Affairs – should consider working collaboratively to develop educational materials that explain clearly to those agents with Powers of Attorney their financial

responsibilities and provide specific examples of what are considered abusive behaviors.

- The U.S. Department of Justice could undertake a study of existing criminal statutes that apply to financial abuse of elders. This should include both federal and state level statutes with the goal to develop a model criminal code applicable to this area that strongly disincents criminal actors and those acting as agents from taking advantage of the elderly.

- Financial institutions are sometimes concerned with the liability they or their employees might incur in situations where they suspect and report elder abuse – particularly if it is a situation in which it is ultimately determined that a fraud was not involved. Today, certain states require the reporting of even suspicions of fraud, but that reporting is not uniform on a national level and statutory hold harmless provisions to protect the reporter seem far from consistent.

  The Council should work toward legislative action that would result in a national reporting statute that provides uniform electronic reporting requirements to a single report point which would disseminate the information (or otherwise make it available) to state and local agencies, as well as uniform hold harmless protections for reporting parties. Additionally, the importance of federal and state agencies such as the CFPB, SEC, FINRA, and NSAA, etc., to coordinate their efforts in addressing elder financial abuse can ensure the avoidance of conflicting rules and regulations, which themselves would potentially harm individual clients. This should also include a definition of those individuals who are protected by the requirements, as in some states fraud of vulnerable adults follow the same requirements as fraud of the elderly.

- Confusion of requirements regarding to whom to report the abuse and under what circumstances.

  FinCEN, a part of the U.S. Treasury, issued an advisory on February 22, 2011 that addresses the reporting of actual or suspected elder financial abuse on Suspicious Activity Reports (SARS).[6] This provided financial institutions with guidance on reporting specific to SARs' requirements; however, the reporting of elder financial abuse often goes beyond that type of reporting. Reporting would likely include reporting of situations to Adult Protective Services or similar agencies as well potentially, depending on the circumstances, to local law enforcement. Today, however, the structure of adult protective services type agencies is diffused across the country. Some locations have more centralized statewide or regional agencies will others structure such agencies very locally. Determining the correct agency for reporting is often difficult. Law enforcement capabilities to deal with such reports often vary as well. In addition, today with law enforcement often done at the local level, it is often difficult to synthesize information across jurisdictions to identify when elders in different locations may be being subjected to scams and fraudulent activity that relates to the same set of criminal actors.

To assist with overcoming these issues, we suggest the following actions:

- The CFPB is currently working with various constituencies to develop a database of regional and local Area Agency on Aging across the United States. Making that database accessible to financial institutions would facilitate those institutions ability to know and contact the correct agency.
- Recognizing that local law enforcement lacked skills in investigating cybercrime, in 2007, the Department of Homeland Security, the United States Secret Service, the Alabama District Attorneys Association, the State of Alabama, and the city of Hoover, Alabama partnered to create the National Computer Forensics Institute (NCFI). This partnership provides state and local law enforcement officers the training necessary to conduct basis electronic crimes investigations. Creating a similar model to train state and local law enforcement personnel the training necessary to conduct investigations of elder abuse could have significant merits. Short of such a large effort, creating and providing to local law enforcement bodies an educational opportunity through such options as written best practices, webinars and seminars on the subject would be beneficial.

  Note that these same concepts can be generally applied as well to local prosecutorial authorities, who sometimes also lack the knowledge and experience requisite to the successful prosecution of those who prey financially on the elderly. Similar training programs and best practices can also serve this community well.
- The CFPB is currently working to establish state and regional coalitions of APS, law enforcement, prosecutors and financial institutions that can work together on the issue of elder abuse. We

encourage continued expansion of this effort and offer our services to assist in connecting our Roundtable members into these coalitions.

- While SARS reporting is working well today, a significant improvement can be made by specifically adding “Elder Financial Abuse” as a category in Section 35 of the SARs Reporting Form. This would allow for easier collation of such activity and facilitate cross matching of potential criminal actors within this area.

- Enhanced financial literacy to empower further consumers, including older Americans, to make sound financial decisions.

  Financial literacy is one of the highest priorities for the Roundtable and its members at the grass roots and at the national policy level. In 2011, Roundtable member companies conducted more than 45,600 financial literacy projects around the country to empower further thousands of consumers to make sound financial decisions.

  As we noted earlier, as a part of the efforts of its Elder Working Group, the Roundtable has committed to work on two projects (i.e., develop a structure/syllabus for training financial institution consumer-facing staff and to develop a publicly available awareness and education program to be made available to all financial institutions).

  We would certainly welcome the engagement of any of the departments or agencies represented on the EJCC in this effort – either in development or ultimately in distribution of the publicly facing awareness and education materials developed. We believe a national-level awareness campaign targeting elder Americans and their family members would provide long-lasting benefits in helping to reduce elder financial abuse.

- One last area of potential improvement involves the licensing of financial professionals who serve the elder community. In its August 20, 2012 letter to the CFPB regarding CFPB’s “Request for Information Regarding Senior Financial Exploitation [Docket CFPB-2012-0018],” the Roundtable mentioned another key area to reduce financial abuse of elders. It noted that an effort to make elders more aware of the licensing of financial professionals coupled with an effort by federal and state agencies and professional organizations’ role in developing best practices for the training and licensing of financial professionals would have benefits. The Roundtable’s comments on this last area are excerpted into Appendix A of this document.

Conclusion

We appreciate the opportunity to share our sector's focus on the issue of financial abuse of the elderly. We are committed to continuing to work on these issues to protect older Americans.

As noted, we recently shared these thoughts with the Elder Justice Coordinating Council. The challenge of reducing elder abuse can only be resolved by continued focus on the issue by all relevant parties, including financial institutions, families of elders, government agencies and legislators. Only through this continued commitment will we be able to protect our seniors from financial abuse. We recognize that the ideas we have outlined in this testimony are, in many cases, concepts and suggestions. They are a starting point for this discussion. We recognize there are various methods to approach these issues and look forward to continuing to work with you and other key constituencies on these issues.

Appendix A

Excerpt from August 20, 2012 letter to the CFPB regarding CFPB's "Request for Information Regarding Senior Financial Exploitation [Docket CFPB-2012-0018]

- Consumers Should Seek Financial Advice Only From Licensed Financial Professionals, and the CFPB Should Work with Federal and State Agencies and Professional Organizations to Develop Best Practices For the Training of These Professionals

The financial services industry has played a vital role in expanding retirement security for millions of Americans for the last 100 years. The industry currently manages more than $17 trillion in retirement assets, which represents 36% of all U.S. household assets.[7] The U.S. retirement market is projected to grow to nearly $22 trillion by 2016,[8] a 30% increase in retirement savings over four years.

It is important that consumers of all ages seek professional assistance to prepare for and make major financial decisions involving investments, wealth planning, and retirement. When making these decisions, consumers should seek out individuals who are licensed under federal and/or state law.

The Roundtable believes that consumers should only hire properly licensed investment professionals. Federal law regulating securities brokers, securities dealers, and investment advisers provides strong and effective protection for all consumers, including older Americans. The Securities and Exchange Commission, together with securities self-regulatory organizations like the Financial Industry Regulatory Authority (FINRA) and the Municipal Securities Rulemaking Board, implement the registration and regulatory régime under federal securities law. These protections are complemented at the state level by laws designed to protect consumers from investment fraud. A similar registration and regulatory structure exists for futures professionals and firms, which are subject to oversight by the Commodity Futures Trading Commission, National Futures Association and other futures self-regulatory organizations. Additionally, state insurance commissioners regulate insurance agents in their respective jurisdictions.[9]

We understand that a number of states and professional organizations have laws and programs that govern certifications and titles used by retirement professionals. While training that focuses on the specialized needs of older Americans may be valuable and useful, we urge the CFPB to partner with the financial services industry, federal regulators, financial industry self-regulatory organizations, state agencies and professional organizations in developing best practices for the training and certification of professionals who specialize in advising older Americans.

End Notes

[1] The Financial Services Roundtable represents 100 of the largest integrated financial services companies providing banking, insurance, and investment products and services to the American consumer. Member companies participate through the Chief Executive Officer and other senior executives nominated by the CEO. Roundtable member companies provide fuel for America's economic engine, accounting directly for $85.5 trillion in managed assets, $965 billion in revenue, and 2.3 million jobs.

[2] The State of Aging and Health in America, Centers for Disease Control and Prevention (CDC) and The Merck Company Foundation, 2007, http://www.cdc.gov/Aging/pdf/saha_2007.pdf.

[3] *The State of Aging and Health in America,* Centers for Disease Control and Prevention (CDC) and The Merck Company Foundation, 2007, *http://www.cdc.gov/Aging/pdf/saha 2007.pdf.*

[4] http://www.consumerreports.org/cro/money/consumer-protection/preventing-financial-elder-abuse/overview/index.htm

[5] BITS - "Protecting the Elderly and Vulnerable from Financial Fraud and Exploitation"

[6] See http://www.fincen.gov/statutes

[7] http://www.ebri.org/research/?fa=genretire

[8] http://www.bankinvestmentconsultant.com/news/cerulli-predicts-retirment-market-will-exceed-22-trillion-by2016-2677132-1.html

[9] The most common license for securities professionals is the Series 7 – General Securities Representative, and the most common license for commodity futures professionals is the Series 3 – National Commodity Futures. Depending on the nature of their activities, investment professionals may need the following licenses: (1) Series 6 – Investment Company Products/Variable Contracts Limited Representative; (2) Series 22 – Direct Participation Programs Limited Representative; (3) Series 31 – Futures Managed Funds; (4) Series 32 – Limited Futures; (5) Series 34 – Retail Off-Exchange Forex; (6) Series 42 – Registered Options Representative; (7) Series 52 – Municipal Securities Representative; (8) Series 62 – Corporate Securities Limited Representative; (9) Series 63 – Uniform Securities Agent State Law (NASAA); (10) Series 65 – Uniform Investment Adviser Law (NASAA); (11) Series 66 – Uniform Combined State Law (NASAA); and (12) Series 82 – Limited Representative, Private Securities Offerings.

In: Financial Exploitation of Elders
Editor: Maxime Faubert

ISBN: 978-1-62417-904-4

Chapter 6

STATEMENT OF PAUL R. GREENWOOD, DEPUTY DISTRICT ATTORNEY, HEAD OF ELDER ABUSE PROSECUTION UNIT, SAN DIEGO DA'S OFFICE*

Good afternoon, Mr. Chairman and distinguished members of the Special Committee on Aging. My name is Paul Greenwood and I have the privilege of heading up the San Diego District Attorney's Office Elder Abuse Prosecution Unit, a position which I have held for the past sixteen years. I am also a co-chair of the California District Attorneys Association Elder Abuse Committee.

California defines an elder as anyone over the age of 65.

I am therefore responsible for prosecuting felony crimes that are committed against victims in that age bracket. These crimes cover physical and mental elder abuse, neglect, and financial exploitation.

At least 65% of my prosecutions involve some form of financial exploitation. The conduct of the criminals is becoming more brazen and diverse. The perpetrators are constantly developing new ways to gain access to our seniors' life savings and have focused upon a generation that typically has been more trusting and less able or willing to self report the victimization.

Let me share some cases to illustrate the problem.

Victoria Gilbert was a convicted felon who moved to San Diego from Nevada. She took a job as a caregiver and started work for an elderly widower

* This is an edited, reformatted and augmented version of testimony given on November 15, 2012 before the Senate Special Committee on Aging.

who was physically and mentally. Within a few days she had convinced the victim to allow her to move in with her boyfriend, Gary Kircus, whom she portrayed as a deputy US Marshall. Soon both Gilbert and Kircus were stealing the victim's medications, and then depleting his checking account and assuming control of his credit card accounts. Fortunately, an alert bank teller became so concerned at the apparent isolation of her customer and the change in banking activity that she contacted the victim's adult children. After making an unannounced visit, the adult daughter discovered her elderly father close to death. Law enforcement was called in and both Gilbert and Kircus were arrested, prosecuted and ultimately convicted after a jury trial.

William Pitre was an unlicensed contractor but described himself in flyers left in church parking lots as a licensed Christian contractor. A 79 year old widow contacted him in response to the flyer left on her car windshield; she wanted her fence repaired and her driveway resealed. The work was shoddy and incomplete; yet Pitre demanded excessive payment. The victim was so fearful that she was unable to write out the checks that Pitre demanded. He wrote out the checks and had the victim sign them. He then left his workmen in the kitchen standing over the victim while Pitre went to the bank to demand cash. The bank became suspicious and called the victim; however she told the bank to give Pitre the cash because she was afraid of what the workmen might do. The victim was too embarrassed to call the authorities; but the bank made a call to Adult Protective Services who in turn contacted law enforcement after visiting the victim. As a result Pitre was arrested and prosecuted and received a state prison commitment.

Donald Wade was a cab driver hired to drive Peggy twice a month to visit with her 93 year old friend Ruth who was in the advanced stages of Alzheimer's and who resided in a skilled nursing facility. On one occasion Peggy cancelled the scheduled visit because of illness; however, Wade seized the opportunity to drive over to the facility and collect Ruth. He drove her to Ruth's bank and along the way obtained Ruth's signature to a CD surrender form that authorized the bank to cash in her CD for $97,000, albeit with a penalty for early withdrawal. Wade convinced the bank to issue a cashier's check payable to Wade's friend whom he described as Ruth's "attorney." At no time did the teller take Ruth to one side and ask her if she understood what was happening. As a result, Wade and his friend were able to steal $96,000 [the bank deducted $1,000 by way of a penalty] from Ruth's account. The crime was only discovered after Wade shot his friend over a dispute as to how the theft proceeds were being divided. Wade was convicted and sentenced to state prison.

These cases underscore the importance of combating financial elder abuse through a multi-disciplinary approach. Throughout California we have seen examples of effective collaboration such as:

1) The emergence of Financial Abuse Specialist Teams [FAST] consisting of representatives from law enforcement, Adult Protective Services, financial institutions, elder law attorneys, prosecutors, and other qualified professionals.
2) The creation of forensic elder centers that offer wrap around services for elder victims; Orange County has led the way thanks to the pioneering efforts of Dr. Laura Mosqueda from the UCI Medical Center.
3) The expansion of mandated reporting to employees of financial institutions who are now required to immediately report suspected elder exploitation to either law enforcement or Adult Protective Services.
4) The implementation of Operation Guardian by the California Attorney General's Office which since the year 2000 has been conducting surprise, on-site inspections of nursing homes. This operation has often led to the uncovering of financial exploitation of residents within a facility in addition to other incidents of neglect.

In San Diego we have tried to replicate this multi-disciplinary concept in the following manner:

1) Periodic lunchtime meetings are held throughout our County to discuss the latest trends and scams - in which we invite community partners to exchange information and receive updates.
2) Trainings for first responders, the clergy and financial institutions in recognizing red flags of elder abuse.
3) Promoting a public awareness campaign entitled "Silence is not golden" – so that the public is encouraged to call a 1-800 number when observing elder abuse
4) Offering comprehensive services to elderly crime victims through our San Diego Family Justice Center and Center for Community Solutions and funded by the not for profit Archstone Foundation.
5) Launching a series of countywide events entitled "Protect yourself and your wallet" that provide education for seniors in the form of tips to avoid becoming a victim of physical and financial abuse. These

seminars are organized by our local Adult Protective Services and the District Attorney's Office and are sponsored by two local Tribal governments. I am attaching to these remarks a copy of my financial exploitation "Top ten tips for seniors".

I am convinced that collaboration by prosecutors with multiple agencies – where the local prosecutor's office takes the initiative – is the key to making an impact on the escalating financial crimes being committed against seniors. There are encouraging signs that prosecutors in several states are capturing the same vision but much more needs to be done. The National Center for State Courts has recently published an excellent resource guide for prosecutors entitled "Prosecuting Elder Abuse cases: Basic Tools and Strategies" funded by the Bureau of Justice Assistance. As more prosecutors take advantage of these training materials, we will see an improvement in how financial elder abuse cases are handled through criminal prosecution.

We also need to eliminate aging discrimination and bias in our attitude towards prosecution of these cases. There has been a tendency in the past for prosecutors to fall into the trap of concluding that:

1) Elders make poor witnesses in court
2) Financial exploitation cases are difficult to prove because of mental capacity issues
3) Cases involving home repair fraud allegations or misuse of Powers of Attorney are best dealt with as civil matters

Prosecutors must find ways to rebut the standard defense that the elder either "loaned" or "gifted" the money to the suspect. Understanding the legal term of consent is at the core of such a case. California crafted a very enlightening jury instruction as follows:

"To consent to a transaction a person must:

- Act freely and voluntarily and not under the influence of threats, force or duress; Have knowledge of the true nature of the act or transaction involved;
- Possess the mental capacity to make an intelligent choice whether or not to do something proposed by another person.
- And consent requires a free will and positive cooperation in act or attitude."

Additionally, prosecutors have to learn how to overcome many elderly victims' reluctance to talk about the exploitation because of embarrassment or fear that such exposure might lead to the victim losing their financial independence.

Moreover, prosecutors should be less concerned about the actual monetary loss and focus more on the underlying conduct by the perpetrator. It is frustrating when a case is rejected by a prosecutor's office because the loss involved does not meet the threshold for prosecution. In my experience, theft of $500 can be as devastating to an elderly widow as a theft of $100,000.

We also should examine ways in which to become more creative and assertive in the actual charges that are filed. For example, consider this hypothetical: An unlicensed contractor fraudulently persuades an elderly homeowner that major corrective work is required on the homeowner's roof. The crook enters the victim's kitchen and stands over the victim while he or she writes out a check. The work is unnecessary, inferior and causes damage to a previously good roof. In that situation we should be looking to not only charge the suspect with elder financial exploitation but also with residential burglary; and if the victim felt intimidated we should consider adding a robbery charge.

Having prosecuted felony financial elder abuse cases for over sixteen years, I see the following areas as crucial in our nation's ability to react to the escalating problem of financial elder abuse:

1) Immediate funding of the Elder Justice Act which was passed over two years ago but which has laid essentially dormant. Much has been achieved at the grass roots level in recent years – but we need some leadership and responsibility from the Federal branch of government in tackling financial elder abuse.
2) We need to look at state laws dealing with elder exploitation. For example, we should be very concerned at the fact that convicted felons can easily get employment working as caregivers. Surely, more can be done to protect the unsuspecting public from hiring felons to look after an aging relative. Additionally, we should evaluate whether state laws relating to financial elder abuse are correctly earmarked as felonies rather than as misdemeanors.
3) We should consider creating or expanding lists of mandated reporters of suspected financial elder abuse. Other logical mandated reporters would be health care workers, first responders, caregivers, medical personnel, the clergy, notary publics and wire transfer merchants.

4) We need to make the court room more elder accessible and learn from such judges as Her Honor Judge Patricia Banks, Presiding Judge of the Elder Law Division in Cook County, Illinois who has gained national attention for the way she operates her Elder courts.
5) All major urban communities should consider having a dedicated investigative law enforcement unit that handles elder abuse investigations. San Diego Police Department has had such a unit since 2000; it consists of five detectives and one sergeant.
6) States should invest in more awareness campaigns so that the public knows exactly how and where to report financial elder exploitation quickly and efficiently.
7) The creation of multi-disciplinary task forces in major urban areas involving federal, state and local law enforcement and adult protective agencies, as well as representatives from financial institutions and wire transfer merchants. Such task forces should be established primarily to provide a rapid response to any report of suspected elder financial exploitation involving an out of state or cross border suspect where monies have been wired. The local prosecutor's office should be willing to seek extradition when a suspect is identified and there is a likelihood of a state prison commitment.
8) The establishing of a national database that tracks different types of elder financial exploitation cases and which offers useful contact information allowing procedures such as obtaining bank records to be expedited.

I last addressed this committee in 2007. Since that time we have made progress both locally and across the country in developing strategies to combat the rising tide of elder exploitation. But I am also aware that the crooks and con artists are becoming more creative and daring in their efforts to deplete the life savings of our senior citizens. It is therefore time for us to go on the offensive in identifying, investigating and prosecuting these suspects. We must expand our multi – disciplinary programs, eliminate misconceptions regarding hurdles to successful prosecution of elder financial abuse, and seek the kind of justice that our seniors deserve.

Paul Greenwood
Deputy District Attorney
Head of Elder Abuse Prosecutions San Diego District Attorneys Office

TEN TIPS TO HELP YOU REDUCE THE RISK OF BECOMING THE NEXT VICTIM OF FINANCIAL ELDER ABUSE

1) CHOOSE A CAREGIVER WITH CAUTION
   Do not assume that by hiring a caregiver through a bonded agency you are guaranteed to get someone who has been checked. There is no current law requiring mandatory background checks for in-home caregivers in California.
2) KEEP AN INVENTORY OF ALL JEWELRY
   Jewelry is the number one item that is stolen from homes occupied by elders. Not only should your jewelry be kept in a locked drawer, you should have photographs of rare, valuable or sentimental items in a separate location. In the event of theft, such photographic evidence will be useful in tracking down the missing jewelry at a pawn shop.
3) EVERY HOME SHOULD HAVE A SHREDDER
   Every piece of mail containing your name, address and any other identifying information should be shredded before being discarded. The most effective type of shredder is the criss-cross cut shredder. Even envelopes with your name and address should be shredded. Never throw away old checkbooks from closed accounts or bank credit card application forms. There is no danger in over shredding!
4) PROTECT YOUR INCOMING AND OUTGOING MAIL
   Never allow incoming mail to sit in an unsecured mailbox where the public have access. Mailbox theft is rampant. Similarly, never leave outgoing mail In an unsecured mailbox with the red flag raised as this simply provides an easy alert to the thief who is cruising the streets. Consider either purchasing a locked mailbox or renting a post office from your local post office.
5) OBTAIN A CREDIT SEARCH ON YOURSELF AT LEAST TWO OR THREE TIMES A YEAR
   Identity theft is rampant. The only way to have peace of mind is to obtain a credit search on yourself periodically from one of the three major credit bureaus – Experian, Equifax and Trans Union. This will enable you to discover whether someone has applied for or obtained a credit card in your name.
6) EVERY TELEPHONE SHOULD HAVE CALLER I.D. FITTED
   All modern telephones are equipped with Caller I.D. capability and the minimal cost of this extra service is well worth it. By seeing if the

incoming call is classified as "private" or "unknown" this will allow you to be immediately on your guard. Crooks love the telephone. It is now their weapon of choice.

7) YOU WILL NEVER WIN THE CANADIAN LOTTERY
If a smooth talking 25 year old male tells you on the telephone that you are the proud winner of the Canadian lottery, he is a liar. Similarly, if you get an email from Nigeria or letter from Madrid indicating that you could receive a substantial amount of money, such communications are always fraudulent. Do not dabble!!

8) CONSIDER ALLOWING YOUR BANK TO SEND A DUPLICATE COPY OF YOUR MONTHLY STATEMENT TO A TRUSTED FAMILY MEMBER OR PROFESSIONAL ADVISOR
Sadly, most financial elder abuse cases are only reported or discovered six to nine months after the initial losses have occurred. Elders whose sight is failing are at greater risk because they may rely upon the very person who is stealing from them to insure that the financial transactions are in order. An independent pair of eyes that is able to look over bank statements every 30 days will be able to catch suspicious activities in the early stages.

9) DON'T ASSUME THAT THE FRIENDLY HANDYMAN IS IN FACT LICENSED
Before committing to any work on your home, always obtain at least three estimates in writing and check on the name of the contractor with both the Better Business bureau and with the State License Contractor's Board. Just because someone gives you an impressive business card with a contractor's license number on it, this does not mean that the person is qualified. The license number may have in fact been stolen. Additionally, never pay more than 10% of the contract price up front.

10) ALWAYS HAVE A SECOND LINE OF DEFENSE AT YOUR FRONT DOOR
You should either have a locked screen door or a security chain guard at your front door. Crooks will attempt to gain entry to your home by using excuses such as a fake emergency, or false uniforms and badges. By having a second line of defense, you will be able to communicate with the stranger on the doorstep without exposing yourself to the possibility of a forced entry. Never allow any stranger into your home even if the emergency seems real. Instead, tell the stranger that you will call 911.

INDEX

A

B

C

D

H

I

J

L

M

N

O

P

Q

R

S

T

U

V

W